C000137816

Thinking Things

General Editors
Graham Slater and C. S. Rodd

9. Is There a God?

Thinking Things Through

Thinking Things Through

9. Is There a God?

C. S. Rodd

EPWORTH PRESS

ISBN 0-7162-0551-3

First published 2002
by Epworth Press
20 Ivatt Way,
Peterborough
PE3 7PG

Typeset by the author
Printed and bound by
Biddles Ltd
Guildford and King's Lynn

Contents

General Introduction

The great Swiss theologian, Hans Küng, has said that his aim in all his writings is to enable his readers to hold their faith with confidence and not with a bad conscience. This new series, prompted by the conviction that Christians need to think through their faith but often lack appropriate help in so doing, has a similar aim. Moreover, the assistance that it seeks to offer is related to another conviction: that many church members need persuading that theologians are concerned in any way with their problems and that theology can be at all relevant to their lives.

In such a situation, it is essential, we are sure, to begin with life and with church life. Only in that way can we be confident that we are dealing with grassroots issues. Plainly, however, it is not enough to identify the questions where they arise; we must also indicate the sources of help – if not of all the answers – in as non-technical a way as possible.

In some volumes, these tasks will be tackled in sequence; in others, they will be interwoven. Whatever the precise format, however, our hope is that, through this interaction, difficulties will be faced, fears dispelled, open discussion promoted, and faith informed and strengthened.

The books can either be read by individuals on their own or used in groups. We hope the questions at the end of each chapter will be useful both as a check that the text has been understood and as a spur to reflection and discussion.

Later volumes will deal with Jesus, the Holy Spirit, and prayer.

GRAHAM SLATER AND C. S. RODD

Introduction

In this book we again meet Anne and Geoff, who were the main characters in my previous books in this series. Tim and Cindy are two new friends. Tim had been an enthusiastic member of Anne's church, but after marrying Cindy, who had long ago given up any belief in God, he came to church less often, stopped being one of the youth leaders, and abandoned training as a lay preacher. Anne is challenged by Cindy to say why she believes in God, and when she struggles to answer this simple question conversations between the friends begin.

Many people are like Cindy. Their own suffering or that of relatives and close friends, the hostile atmosphere created by science, technology, and the market economy, and the assumptions behind many television programmes make it hard for them to maintain their faith. They are not necessarily opposed to religion, but none of the arguments for the existence of God satisfies them any longer.

Others are like Tim. They used to be enthusiastic church members, but pressures of work and new friendships have weakened their links with the church and the support they received from their Christian community. They have not explicitly rejected religious belief, but God no longer seems important in their lives. They discover, perhaps to their surprise, that they can get on quite well without him.

Others again are like Anne. She genuinely believes and goes to church to worship God, but when asked to give a reason for her faith, she finds that she has no answer – and this troubles her.

Yet others have had religious experiences which make it impossible for them *not* to believe. Fred, another character from my previous books, belongs to this group, and, as a result, he is more interested in living out his faith than in discussing religious issues. But, as the friends talk, they can never forget him.

As the discussions proceed, the friends discover that at the heart of the problem lies the question What kind of God do you believe in (or reject)?

Once again I am deeply grateful to Graham Slater for his co-operation over this series and especially for his constant encouragement during the time of writing this book. As with my earlier books, he has been a most enthusiastic supporter, and a gentle but firm critic of my style. I am also grateful to Gerald Burt and G. W. S. Knowles for reading the text and offering perceptive and helpful comments. I must point out that I alone am responsible for the ideas expressed in it.

C. S. RODD

Part 1

The Friends

1
Tim Stops Coming to Church

Anne was worried about Tim. It was four weeks now since he last came to church. What was wrong? He used to be one of the keenest members. He taught in Junior Church. He was one of the leaders in the youth group and the group was growing quite dramatically. He played both organ and drums very well, and somehow he managed to please nearly everyone with the music he chose. He had even started to train as a lay preacher, and the couple of services that he had taken were really inspiring.

For some time, Anne knew, pressures had been building up at work. His company had been taken over, and the new firm had carried out a 'downsizing' exercise. Everyone was working flat out in the hope that they wouldn't be selected for compulsory redundancy.

Moreover, Tim had recently married Cindy. Anne wasn't sure where they'd met. She only knew that Cindy didn't go to church anywhere. The only time she did come with Tim was soon after they'd got to know each other, and although she wanted to please Tim and smiled politely at everyone, it was pretty clear that she equated Christianity with superstition and didn't want to have anything to do with it.

At first, Tim's absences from worship because of work only affected the odd Sunday, and he would return as cheerful and energetic as ever. It was true that, after a while, he abandoned the preachers' training course, saying that, with the pressures at work, he simply didn't have time. In other ways, however, his commitment seemed undiminished. But now he'd been missing for four weeks, and no one seemed to know why. Several blamed Cindy for leading him astray.

Anne knew that some people were concerned about Tim and perhaps a bit disappointed in him. She was also aware that they didn't know how to handle the present situation and so it was unlikely that anyone had been round to see him. So she decided to go herself.

Tim was rather embarrassed. 'Nice of you to come,' he said. Cindy was far less welcoming. She made it pretty clear, in fact, that she regarded Anne's visit as an intrusion. Coffee was produced – by Tim. They talked about this and that – the nice flat, the lovely curtains, the daring pictures on the walls – with long pauses in between. At last they got round to Tim's work, and he explained that it was absorbing all his time and energy so that, on those Sundays when he was free, he simply wanted to rest at home. Cindy remained silent.

Anne left fairly soon and, as she walked home, she felt very depressed. She hadn't discovered the real reason why Tim hadn't been to church. She hadn't managed to show Cindy that she just wanted to be friends and wasn't going to try to convert her. It was a complete fiasco, and she began to wish she hadn't gone.

She was very surprised, therefore, when on the following evening she had a phone call from Tim. Could he and Cindy come round to her home for a chat, he asked. Relieved that she had decided against going to a concert, she told him, in as welcoming a tone as she could manage, that she would be delighted to see them. 'Come as soon as you like,' she said. 'I'm on my own all evening.'

After they had settled down to coffee and cake, it was Cindy who started the conversation. She apologized for being so sullen the day before, and added: 'You couldn't help seeing that I resented your coming round, and yet you didn't let it affect the friendly way you spoke to both of us. And I'd like you to know I appreciated that.'

Anne felt rather embarrassed, and not knowing what to say, just said nothing. Then Tim spoke. 'After you went last night,' he said, 'we talked for a very long time. You see, what with work and those trips abroad for the firm, life truly has been very hectic. Even so, I felt bad about not coming to church. But when I did come, I felt a certain coolness from some of the church members. It made me wonder if I was really welcome.'

Anne poured out another cup of coffee, and then said, 'But why have you come round now? It wasn't just to apologize for last night, was it?'

'No,' said Cindy. 'You see, when I met Tim and discovered that he went to church, I was horrified. But we agreed to differ. He could go to church, and I wouldn't object. As you know, I came with him once, and that was enough. I was pleased, I admit, when he missed going some Sundays – one trip, in fact, wasn't strictly for his firm! But then, after you came round to see us last night, we talked and talked, and agreed that we would ask you if we could come round tonight. So here we are.'

Anne was still puzzled. What had she said that made Cindy and Tim want to come to see her? So she did what she had learnt to do when things were a bit beyond her. She came straight out with what she was thinking. 'I thought it was pretty dismal last night. I didn't feel that I was particularly friendly or anything . . .' She trailed off. 'That's just it,' Cindy exclaimed. 'You didn't push religion. You didn't try to convert me. You didn't go on at Tim for not coming to church. You were just . . . nice.'

'Cindy's left out something rather important,' Tim said. 'One of the things we talked about last night was whether there is a God. I'd better confess. I've been having doubts recently. Oh, you'll say it's Cindy's influence, but it isn't that at all. As you know, I've always come to church since I was a boy in the Sunday School. And I liked doing all the things that I did. Playing the organ and the drums put me in the limelight. I get on well with kids, and running the youth club was fun. And I took religion for granted. I suppose I believed in a way. But I hadn't thought it through. This last month I've thought about God more than I did in all the years that I've been coming to church. Odd, isn't it? All those years I was coming to church I didn't really think about what I was doing, but when I stopped coming I began to think seriously about God. And then you came round last night and Cindy and I talked about God for the first time. Seriously, that is. And we both decided that we wanted to talk it over with you.'

'Why me?' thought Anne. But she said, 'Fine. Where do we begin.'

'Well,' said Cindy, 'why do you believe in God?'

There was silence. Anne had never been asked that question straight out before – and she didn't know the answer. At last, deciding that honesty was the only thing that Cindy would accept, she said, 'I've never been asked that before. And I don't know.'

'There,' said Cindy to Tim, 'I knew I was right. I told you that Anne would give an honest answer. I'm so glad I persuaded you to come to see her. At last I think I've found someone who won't put me off with pious claptrap.' She looked at the clock. 'It's getting late. Look, do you have the time to come for a serious talk about religion this time next week? We'd love to have you for a meal.' She gave Anne a sly look. 'And you'll have seven days to cook up an answer to my question.'

Questions for discussion

1. Why do *you* believe in God?

2. How honest have you been about your real beliefs?

3. What is your reaction to Tim and Cindy?

2

Talk Over a Meal

Anne had a miserable week. Cindy's question kept running round and round in her head, like a tune that you can't stop humming. Why did she believe in God? Honestly, she didn't know. Some of the people at church had had religious experiences. She'd never had one. Not a real one, that is. She'd sometimes felt a kind of glow during a service, but she put it down to emotion. She remembered the time when she had been cycling home through the lanes on a summer evening and seen the shadows across the hills, and suddenly she had a feeling that was more than just a sense of the beauty of nature. But she explained that as emotion too. She'd never had an experience of God's presence. She supposed she'd just taken God's existence for granted.

She puzzled over Cindy's question every time she was on her own. She thought back. She remembered the difficulties she'd found in the Bible, and how Geoff had helped her to adopt a relaxed attitude to it. But there had never been any question about whether there was a God. She recalled the problems she'd had about the evil and suffering in the world – but again she'd taken God's existence for granted. The difficulty was in trying to reconcile a loving God with the suffering that she'd come up against. She'd never questioned whether God actually existed. She thought about the way even Geoff had seemed out of his depth when it came to believing in life after death – but again, he was firmly convinced of the existence of God. It seemed as if God was the solid ground on which they'd based all their other beliefs. And now there was Cindy's question!

Friday came, and she found herself ringing the bell at Cindy's flat. How much warmer the welcome was than the first time she'd rung that bell. They had their drinks, learnt a bit more about each other, and went in to a marvellous meal. Half-way through Cindy looked hard at Anne and said: 'You haven't

7

found the answer to my question, have you?' 'How did you know?' said Anne, surprised. 'I could tell from the way you were trying to talk about everything else except my question,' she answered.

'No,' said Anne, 'you're quite right. I haven't managed to "cook up an answer".' They all laughed, and Cindy said, 'Good for you! Now we all start at level pegging. Come and sit in a comfortable chair, while I bring the coffee, and then we'll see what you do have to say for yourself.'

After they were settled, Anne said, 'Well, I may as well tell you that I haven't been able to get away from your wretched question all week. The more I've thought about it, the more I realize that I just don't know why I believe in God.' And then she went on to tell them about the way she had been thinking about religious experiences, and about the people in church who seemed to be having them at least once a Sunday, some of them every day. One member had told her that he'd stopped listening to the Today programme on the car radio as he drove to work and talked to Jesus instead. 'And he meant it. It was not just a pious way of saying he prayed. He actually felt that Jesus was with him in the car.' But Anne had never had an experience at all like that. She told them about the emotional feelings that she had remembered as she'd been thinking about Cindy's question during the week, and said that she would never think of calling them experiences of God.

'I suppose,' Tim said, 'that if you'd had a real experience of God, that would be that. You wouldn't be able to doubt God's existence ever again. Anne, do you remember that minister who told us of the time he'd actually seen Jesus? He said that he'd been out with his girl friend and had come back to her home for supper. Both of them knew that the feelings they had for each other had slowly died, but they didn't know how to break off their relationship. Suddenly, while she was in the kitchen and he was laying the table, he turned round and saw Jesus standing in front of him. Jesus looked at him, and then vanished without

8

saying a word. It was so real that he almost shouted out, "Come back and tell me what you came for." He told us that he knows that Jesus came to give him the grace to break with his girl friend. Within a week she'd met her future husband, and he'd met his future wife. The minister told us that he will never forget that night.'

'Oh, come on,' Cindy retorted, 'How did your minister know it was Jesus? If he had been a Catholic I expect it would have been the Virgin Mary that he saw. He was just emotionally stirred up and had an hallucination. Don't you agree, Anne? You've been honest about your feelings. You admitted that what you felt was just emotion. It was just like that with that minister.'

'But the people who say they've had these experiences of God are absolutely convinced about it,' said Anne. 'So they may be,' Cindy replied, 'but that doesn't prove that what they felt were actually experiences of God. It only means that they had experiences which they interpreted as being experiences of God. They might have been caused by any number of things. Just like Anne's feeling about the beauty of those hills and shadows in the evening sun.'

'Perhaps we're expecting a religious experience to be more dramatic than it actually is,' said Tim. 'Mightn't it be that it is something much quieter. Fred – he's one of our older members,' he explained to Cindy – 'Fred told me of the time just after his wife died and he felt utterly alone and almost in despair, and suddenly a strange kind of peace came over him. He said he couldn't describe it. It wasn't any kind of vision, and he didn't hear a voice or feel a hand placed on his shoulder. He simply knew that God was with him, and that everything would be all right.' Anne was glad that Cindy didn't immediately rubbish that. She had great respect for Fred. She knew that he loved his Lord, as he used to put it, and she was certain that he had no doubts at all about that experience of peace. And yet . . .

9

They'd been silent for some time, when Cindy said, 'I can respect that. And I'm willing to admit that I can't explain what produced that sense of peace. For *him* that would be sufficient to make him certain of God. But it isn't *proof.* We don't know, and someone else's experience can't provide any grounds for us to believe in God.'

It was getting late, and Anne suggested they should meet at her home next week. 'I won't put on anything like the splendid meal that you gave me tonight. If we are going to meet regularly once a week we must take each other as we really are. But I'd like to ask Geoff to come as well.' Cindy was about to object, when Tim put his hand on her arm and said, 'You'll like Geoff. You really will. He's a bit like Anne. I'm sure that you'll enjoy arguing with him.' So it was agreed.

Questions for discussion

1. If you've had any religious experiences, how do they confirm your faith in God? If you have never had any experience of God, in what ways can the experiences of other people point to God's existence?

2. Why do you think some people lose their faith?

3. What answer can you give to the argument that religious experiences are just emotion?

3

What Do You Mean by 'God'?

Next week Anne laid on a simple meal of sandwiches and a trifle she had made. At first the going was a bit difficult. Geoff was never one for small talk and kept pretty quiet. Cindy wasn't sure that she could trust him. Suppose he started to try to convert her? Anne began to wish she hadn't suggested asking him to join them. It looked as if it was going to be very sticky, and it wasn't until they were drinking their coffee that she plucked up sufficient courage to start the serious discussion.

She explained to Cindy and Tim that she'd told Geoff what they'd been discussing last week, and then, turning directly to Geoff, she said, 'So why do you believe in God?' She wasn't surprised when Geoff replied with another question: 'What do you mean by "God"?'

'Well . . . God . . . ,' she answered, rather tamely. Then she was silent.

Geoff allowed the silence to go on for quite a long time, and then said, 'I'm sure that Cindy here will say that it doesn't make much sense to ask anyone why they believe in God if you don't know what you are asking them to say they believe in.' He gave a grin, and Cindy grinned back.

Tim began to feel sorry for Anne, and he said: 'We all know what we mean when we say we believe in God, surely?' 'Well?' asked Geoff. Now it was Tim's turn to be embarrassed. 'I certainly don't believe in an old man in the sky', he said. 'Oh, I thought you did,' said Cindy, with a laugh. Then she suddenly became serious. 'How about all that talk about our being made in the image of God? The minister went on and on about it that time I came to church with you. Doesn't that really mean that we make God in our own image? There was that old Greek philosopher who said that if horses had hands and could

11

draw they would draw the gods in the form of horses.[1] And we read a poem at school once about the kind of God fish would believe in. I think it was called 'Heaven'. I can't remember who wrote it, but I can still remember a couple of lines:

> And under that Almighty Fin
> The littlest fish might enter in.[2]

That's why I can't believe in God. I think it's just wishful thinking, and people invent the kind of God who will comfort them, and then they call him Father.'

Anne wasn't going to let her get away with this. 'I certainly don't believe that we are made in God's image, at least not in the way you are thinking,' she said. 'I accept evolution, so that I don't believe that God made human beings in his image – if that has any meaning at all. I certainly don't take Genesis literally.'

'So what is your idea of God?' Geoff asked.

Anne thought, and then she said, 'I suppose I do think of him as human in a sort of way. After all, how else can you think of God? But I know that God is a spirit, and is more than just a "person". But if he wasn't "personal" in some way, how could we pray to him?'

'So you think of God as an individual, though not just as a human being, but more magnificent and powerful and good?' said Geoff. 'That's right,' Anne replied. 'Something like that. And of course although I say 'he' and 'him' I don't think of him as a man.' She paused, and then added, 'Or perhaps I do. How can you think of a person without thinking of them as either a man or a woman. But I know inside that he is not male – or female.'

---

[1] Xenophanes: 'But if cattle and horses or lions had hands, or were able to draw with their hands and do the works that men can do, horses would draw the forms of the gods like horses, and cattle like cattle, and they would make their bodies such as they each had themselves' (from G. S. Kirk and J. E. Raven, *The Presocratic Philosophers*, CUP, 1957, 169).
[2] Rupert Brooke, *Heaven*.

'That's how I think of God too,' said Tim. 'If he were not a person, wouldn't he be less than we are, not greater?'

'So Cindy is right,' said Geoff. 'You simply picture God as a human being, though better and greater and "spiritual", whatever that may mean.'

Cindy now spoke up. 'You think I'm just a pagan,' she said, 'but I *have* read one or two books, you know. And I discovered that some theologians say that everything we can say about God is metaphorical. He is actually outside time and space, but apart from that nothing that people say about him can be taken literally. We cannot know what God is like in himself.'

Tim was rather impressed. Although he'd known Cindy for quite a long time and they'd been married for nearly six months, he hadn't realized that she had ever thought seriously about religion. Cindy guessed what he was thinking. 'Oh yes,' she said, looking over to him, 'I don't go to church – I never have – you know that. But I did read a bit about religion when I was in the sixth form at school. I think all this business of analogy and metaphor is nonsense. If you can't say anything definite about God, what can you really know about him? Nothing, as far as I can see. You can't know that your metaphors are like him at all.'

Anne was puzzled. 'I'm not sure I understand what you are talking about,' she said. '"Analogy" and "metaphor" – what is that all about?'

Cindy thought hard, and then she said: 'I think that what the philosophers in the books that I read at school meant is something like this. The only thing that we can say literally about God – if there is a God – is that he is outside of space and time. Nothing else that we say about him is literally true. Take "Our Father". God didn't literally enter into sexual relations with our mothers and beget us. What is meant is that God is *like* a father.'

'I can see that,' Anne said. 'But if God is "like a father", doesn't that really mean that he is a Father?' She was silent, for

13

a moment. 'No, I don't quite mean that. I mean that if he is "like a father" he will do the kind of things a father would do. So in a sense he *is* a Father.'

'I don't think you quite see what I mean,' Cindy replied. 'Look at it another way. We say that our neighbour is "friendly" and that the dogs over the road are "friendly", and that the new computer programme that we have just bought is "user friendly". But 'friendly' means three different things, and we can distinguish them quite easily, because we know people and dogs and computers and we make adjustments in the meaning of "friendly". I might even say to my little nephew, "Say hello to Mr Brown. He won't bite."' They laughed.

Anne could understand this, but she still didn't quite see what it had to do with being able to talk about God. Cindy tried to explain. 'We know what slant we have to give to the word "friendly" because we are familiar with dogs and people and computers. We know that "friendly" dogs will wag their tails and try to lick our face. They won't bite us. We also know that the computer is just a machine, so that although the programmer produced a program that we find easy to use, neither the computer nor the program have any feelings at all. They do not regard us a friends. So "friendly" really means three different things. We can use the same word because we have met people and dogs and own a computer, and so know what meaning we have to give to the word. This is what philosophers mean by "analogy".'

Anne began to see what Cindy was driving at, but it seemed terribly complicated. Most people called dogs 'friendly' without thinking much about it, and when they said their computer program was 'user friendly' they said it almost as a joke. And she was still not sure what it had to do with the kind of God she believed in.

So Cindy went on: 'We can't see God, or touch him. He can't speak to us, because he doesn't have a body. So if we say that God is 'friendly' we don't know what kind of meaning we should give to the word. We know that 'friendly' must have a different meaning from what it means when we use it of human beings and dogs and computers, because God is not a human being or a dog or a computer. The trouble is that analogy only works when you know both what it literally applies to (human beings) and what it applies to by analogy (dogs and computers). You say that God is personal. But suppose that he is really a massive computer. That was why I said that you cannot know that what you say about God has any real meaning.'

Anne still wasn't totally convinced. She pointed out that although we don't know what God is like, as Tim said, we know that he must at least be like a person, because that is the highest form of life that we know. So that when we say that God is 'loving', we think of the most loving actions and the most loving people that we know, and we say that God is like that – only much, much more.

This didn't satisfy Cindy. 'You said that God is "the highest form of life that we know", but the only "life" we know is on earth. And if God exists at all, he must be so much greater than we are that it is bound to be impossible for us to say anything about him that we can suppose is remotely certain.'

She went on: 'How about that Church of England priest who lost his job at a theological college because he said that God didn't "exist" in the same way as things exist in our world, but he still believed in the importance of goodness, love, truth and wisdom. He claims that he's still a Christian, but as far as I can see he's an atheist. He doesn't believe that there is a God – not the kind of God any ordinary person would regard as God. For him "God" is a human invention. He may still use the word, but it means no more than the sum of all his values and ideals.'[3]

Anne and Tim were inclined to agree with her, but Geoff said, 'Hold on. Suppose you thought that Christians believe in a

---

[3] The priest is Antony Freeman. He has set out his beliefs in *God In Us: A Case for Christian Humanism* (SCM Press, 1993).

God who *is* "an old man in the sky", or something like that. A kind of glorified human being – male, naturally – who made the world and all the animals and men and women in six days. A God who helps Christians out of difficulties, if they only believe in him strongly enough. A God who takes good Christians to heaven and sends everyone else to hell. Suppose that is what you think you have to believe in if you're to be a Christian, and you simply can't believe any of it. Would you be an atheist?'

'Of course not,' Anne replied, rather sharply. 'Anyone who had that picture of God and found it impossible to believe in him is just rejecting a false idea of God. They might even believe in God if they had the right idea of what God is like.'

'Good', said Geoff. 'So whether you are an "atheist" or not depends on what idea you have of the God you are rejecting.' Tim and Anne supposed that that was so. 'Right,' Geoff went on, 'now let's try to imagine how that Anglican priest was thinking. Perhaps he came to believe that human beings worked out their ideas of God for themselves. They described God as all-good, all-loving, all-wise. "Because he's God," they said, "he must be immortal. And obviously he is invisible." When the priest no longer believed that there was a supernatural God, he was really saying that we can never discover whether God "exists" or not. But he still believed that goodness, love, and wisdom are real and that they matter. So all he was saying was that instead of trying to believe in a God whom it was impossible to know about, he believed in the value of goodness, and so on, and tried to live by those ideals.'

'I still don't see that he can be described as anything else but an atheist,' said Anne. 'After all, he doesn't believe that God exists, does he?' Geoff agreed that this was probably true, but he wondered whether it made much difference to the way he lived.

Still puzzled, Anne said, 'Well then, how can we decide whether God exists or not?' Cindy looked at Geoff, who said,

'That's too big a question to start on tonight. Come round to my place next week and we'll see what we can do about it.'

Questions for discussion

1. What picture of God do you have?

2. Geoff said that whether anyone was properly described as an atheist depended on the idea of God that he or she rejected. Are there any ideas about God that you reject?

3. What difference does it make to the way we live whether we believe that God exists or not?

4

Anne Meets Sarah

Anne was surprised and delighted. She was doing some shopping in the market place and suddenly bumped into Sarah. She hadn't seen Sarah for ages, not since Sarah had left the church because she said she wasn't going to listen to the nonsense that many male preachers talked in the pulpit. 'If God is male, then male is god,' she had said, and left the church.

She seemed quite pleased to see Anne again, and after they had chatted for some time, and caught up on their news, Sarah said, 'Come and have coffee in that lovely little coffee shop overlooking the river.' As they drank their coffee Anne found herself telling Sarah about the discussions she was having with Cindy, Tim and Geoff. She was full of the previous evening when they had talked about the kind of God they believed in. 'You should have been there,' she said; 'you could have set us right about a male God!'

Sarah laughed. 'No,' she said, 'I don't think I would have fitted in. But I'll tell you what I think about God. I've come a long way since we last met,' and she went on to explain that she had come to see that it wasn't just a matter of speaking of God as 'Mother' as well as 'Father' – or even instead of 'Father'. It wasn't good enough to emphasize that Jesus became 'human' rather than 'a man', since he was still *male*. All the words that Christians use about God are male. They are concerned with things like power and authority and domination. Christianity has encouraged men to dominate and destroy the natural world. The whole Christian tradition has to be abandoned. We have to find a completely new way of thinking about God.

Anne was intrigued. 'What new way is there?' she asked.

Sarah enthusiastically began to set out the new beliefs that she'd come to accept. 'I've come to see that the only way forward for women and for the world is to base our religion on women's experience. We have to begin from women's bodies, not from the male phallus, erect, strong, hard.' Anne was amused, but tried not to show it, for Sarah was deadly serious. Sarah continued, 'If we women are to escape from exploitation and give a future to the world, we must have a Goddess who is one of us and who is part of a green world.' She explained that she was not interested in a Goddess who was simply a female God. When she spoke of Goddess she was referring to an attitude to the world, an attitude of liberation for all those who are being exploited. 'Goddess is an ecologically harmonious world. Goddess is creative self-expression.'

Anne was feeling completely out of her depth, and began to wonder whether Sarah was simply being intoxicated with words. But Sarah went on. 'For me, Goddess is starving to death in refugee camps. Goddess is a ten year old girl forced into prostitution. Goddess is the animals being destroyed in the rain forests. Goddess is the whole suffering world.'

The waitress was looking anxiously at them, and they had to pay the bill and go. They made no arrangement to meet again. Anne felt that Sarah had moved so far away from the faith that she herself held that they now had little in common. The groups to which she now belonged seemed exotic, if not a little mad. But it had been an interesting encounter.[1]

Questions for discussion

1. What is your reaction to the complaint that Christianity is too patriarchal?

2. In what ways do you think that 'women's experience' leads to new ways of thinking about God?

---

[1] I am indebted for much of this to Beverley Clack and Brian R. Clack, *The Philosophy of Religion: A Critical Introduction* (Polity Books, 1998).

5

How Do We Decide Whether God Exists?

The next week they were all ready to get down to the discussion straight away. They'd all been puzzling over the question that they'd ended up with last time: How can we decide whether God exists or not? That is, all except Cindy, who had already decided that there wasn't a God. But she and Tim had agreed that they wouldn't discuss religion between themselves. 'I want to think it out for myself,' he told her. 'You'll persuade me to think like you do.' The trouble was that he didn't know where to begin, and he was pleased to find that Anne didn't know either. Geoff suggested that perhaps it would be a good idea to ask Cindy why she didn't believe in God.

She explained that at school she had been interested in religion in a rather detached way, and had read about several arguments for the existence of God. None of them had convinced her. In fact, she was surprised that any philosophers had taken them seriously.

Anne had never heard of 'arguments for the existence of God' and she asked Cindy to explain.

'Take that stupid argument,' she said, 'about that "than which no greater can be conceived". You first define God as a being who is more perfect than any other that we can imagine. Then you say that an imaginary God is less perfect than a God who exists. So he must exist. I ask you! Just because you can imagine something that is perfect doesn't mean that it exists. I can imagine a perfect island, with glorious beaches, palm trees, sunshine and cool breezes – but that doesn't mean that I shall ever find one outside of the travel brochures.'

Anne and Tim had never met that argument before, and they weren't quite sure that they'd understood it, but as Cindy set it out it seemed as stupid to them as it did to her. But surely, if great philosophers had proposed it, it couldn't just be stupid. Geoff realized that they hadn't seen the point. 'The point is,' he said, 'that the man who invented this argument hadn't really understood the logic of what he was saying. Look at it like this,' he went on. 'What is the difference between an "existing cow" and a "non-existing cow"?' 'That's easy,' Anne immediately responded. 'An "existing" cow is one that really exists, and a "non-existing cow" is one that doesn't.' Cindy laughed. 'But if a "non-existing cow" doesn't exist,' she said, 'how do you know that it's a cow?'

'Well,' Anne replied, 'I know what a cow is, and if there was a field without a cow in it, that, I suppose, would be a "non-existing" one.' 'But why isn't it a "non-existing sheep" in the field instead of a "non-existing cow"?' Tim could see that Anne was getting a bit flustered, and he interrupted with, 'It's all pretty silly really. There isn't such a thing as a "non-existing" anything. We are just playing with words. I think we ought to get back to why we believe that there is a God.'

'Hold hard,' said Geoff. 'It may seem stupid to talk about a "non-existing" cow, but how about a "non-existing unicorn"?' 'What are you getting at now?' Tim asked. 'Well,' Geoff said, 'put it like this. We know that cows can exist, even if there isn't one in Anne's empty field, and we know that unicorns don't exist. They're just imaginary animals. But that doesn't mean that you cannot find a picture of one. When I was quite little I had a book of all kinds of animals, and there was a magnificent picture of a unicorn in it.'

'What's all this got to do with "non-existing" cows and whether God exists?' Anne asked.

'Just this,' Geoff explained. 'We have an idea of a cow or a unicorn. If we are clever enough we could even draw them. Certainly we've seen pictures of what they're like (or what they're supposed to be like). But if we want to know whether they exist or not, we have to go round and see whether we can find one. Of course, even if we don't find one, it doesn't mean that they don't exist. It's just that we haven't found one *yet*. Though since most of the world has now been explored

21

we can be pretty sure that we're not going to come across a unicorn.'

Anne was still puzzled. 'But what's all this got to do with whether God exists or not,' she asked. Geoff explained. 'You were quite right to say that it makes no sense to talk about a "non-existing cow". It *is* just playing with words. Or perhaps I ought to say that it is *misunderstanding* the words. I can speak of a brown cow or a black and white cow, because "brown" and "black and white" describe the cow. But "existing" doesn't describe the cow at all. I can go out and look for a black and white Friesian cow, because that is the kind of cow I'm trying to find. But I can't go out to look for a "non-existing" cow (or an "existing" one for that matter). At first sight it looks as if "non-existing" is an adjective just like "black and white", but it isn't really.'

'All right,' Anne admitted, 'I think I can understand that, but I still don't see what it has to do with whether God exists or not.'

During this discussion Tim had sat silent. At first he appeared to be just as confused as Anne, but now his face lit up. He turned to Geoff. 'Is this what you are getting at? You can't have an "existing God" any more than you can have an "existing cow". And if that is so, then you can't say that an "existing God" is greater or more perfect than a "non-existing" one.'

'That's right,' Geoff replied. Then he added, 'But it isn't quite as simple as that.' The others all groaned. 'Go on,' said Tim, 'tell us the worst.'

'It's like this,' Geoff continued. 'We saw that to find out whether unicorns exist or not you have to have an idea of what a unicorn is like, and then you go out and look for one. Or if you think that is too fanciful, you might say that if you want to know whether there are any cows in New Zealand you go out there to see whether you can find one. But you know what it is you're looking for because you know what a cow is.'

22

Suddenly Anne saw what he was driving at. 'What you mean is that we have to have an idea of God before we can decide whether there is a God or not. Is that right?'

'Yes,' Geoff replied, 'and that's why I said last week that whether you are an "atheist" or not depends on what picture of God you are rejecting. That's why it's important first of all to decide what we mean by "God".'

He went on, 'And there's another thing. Although we have agreed that it makes no sense to talk about an "existing God" as greater than a "non existing" one, perhaps being able *not* to "not exist" – in other words, to exist always – is an important part of what we mean by God. Unless he was "always" there he wouldn't be God. But, of course, "always" is only our way of speaking. What we really mean is that he would somehow be there even before our universe of time and space existed, and he will still be there when the universe runs down and all life becomes extinct.'

By this time Anne had become quite excited. 'So the argument isn't quite as pointless as Cindy claimed, and . . .', when Tim noticed that Cindy looked a little put out, and he quickly interrupted, 'No, I wouldn't say that. It's obvious that as an *argument* to try to prove that God exists it has failed. So Cindy was right. But it has shown us a little more about what kind of a God we're looking for. And I think that that is quite useful.'

A smile came over Cindy's face. 'Yes, I suppose that's about it. But how about the other arguments that I discovered.'

Geoff looked at his watch. 'It's too late to start on those now,' he said. 'Better pack up for the night. Who's going to invite us next week?' 'It's our turn,' Cindy and Tim shouted out together.

Questions for discussion

1. Are you sure you have really understood the argument? If not, try to set it out in your own words. Or let someone else in the group try to explain it.

2. Why did Geoff say that although the argument was invalid, it had important things to teach us?

3. Once again we've seen that it's important to know what kind of a God we are believing in. What more have you learnt about him from tonight's discussion?

6
The Watchmaker: Blind or Not?

They settled down very quickly, all of them eager to get on with the discussion they'd left off last week. Geoff looked at Cindy. 'What argument are you going to knock down today?'

'What about Paley's watch,' she replied. 'Everyone has heard about that, haven't they?' Anne had heard of it, but didn't know what it was, so she asked Cindy to explain.

'What Paley said was that if we found a watch on a beach and picked it up, we would say that someone must have made it. With all those cogs and wheels and the hands and a spring to make it go, it couldn't just have happened by chance. There had to be a maker. So there must be a God to make the universe, which is far more complicated than a watch. It couldn't just have happened by chance.'

'It sounds convincing to me,' said Anne.

'Oh, come on,' retorted Cindy, 'you can't really swallow that one can you? Haven't you heard of the Blind Watchmaker?'

'Tell us more,' said Tim. So Cindy explained to them that the idea that the world was like a watch and so there had to be a clever watchmaker had been destroyed by evolution. When Anne still looked puzzled, Cindy pointed out that before Darwin people could assume that God had given fish their streamlined shape so that they could swim easily in the water. He had made giraffes with long necks so that they could eat the leaves from the tops of the trees. He had created the swallow so that it could fly swiftly and catch insects. He had made eyes for animals and human beings so that they could see to get their food and enjoy the world. And so on. But now we know that instead of animals having been created with special characteristics to enable them to live in their environment, these features developed by way of random changes and natural selection over many millions of years. Everything in the world just happened by chance. Instead of a clever 'Watchmaker', there is just the 'Blind Watchmaker', blind chance. Evolution just happened, and the reason why creatures seem specially designed for where they live is because those that developed characteristics that made it more likely that they would survive long enough to breed passed on those characteristics to their offspring. But the changes were pure chance. And even that wasn't the end of it. Scientists have now shown us that in the end all plants and animals live simply in order that the genes can continue to live on from one animal or person to another. 'It isn't just that it all happened by chance, so that there is no need to suppose that a God created it, but it's all pretty pointless as well,' she ended.

'So that argument's done for!' said Tim.

Anne was very upset. 'But if we can't argue that the world is so intricate that there must be a God to create it, can't we say that the whole universe is so wonderful that it couldn't just have happened by chance? It's here, when it might not be. So there must be a Creator.'

'Hold on,' said Geoff, 'don't rush so quickly. There are several things you've both overlooked.' They all turned to him. 'Like what?' Cindy asked.

'Well,' Geoff went on, 'have you ever considered how probable it is that the universe just happened by chance, Cindy?' 'Oh, that's easy,' she replied. 'Even if it is hugely improbable, given long enough time (if it's sensible to talk about time), it could have appeared in the end.'

Geoff wasn't going to let her off so lightly. 'All right,' he said, 'I'll allow you vast tracts of time, so long in fact that we can hardly call it time at all. But it still seems to me to make more sense to say that some personal being created the universe than that it just evolved by pure chance.'

Tim had been looking puzzled for some time, and now that there was a pause in the conversation he broke in. 'I'm not clear about what the point of the argument is.' 'How so?' said Cindy. 'Well,' he replied, 'it seems to me that we are really talking about two different things. When Paley spoke about the watch and the watch-maker, he seemed to be thinking of how intricate the universe is, and how similar it was to something that human beings make. So only someone with a mind and a purpose could have made it. But now we seem to be arguing about whether the universe could exist just of itself or whether there had to be a Creator. Aren't these two different arguments?'

They all agreed that Tim had a point. 'So where do we go from here?' he said.

˙ 'I think,' Geoff said, 'we should go back to Paley's argument. Oh, I know that Cindy has no time for it, but I wonder whether there might be something in it after all.' 'You mean like that argument that we talked about last week?' Anne asked. 'Yes,' Geoff replied, 'but not in quite the same way. Last week we decided that although the argument about an "existing God" didn't prove anything, it helped us to see a little more clearly what we mean by "God". But the point about Anne's argument is that, if you set it out a little differently, it does make sense.'

Cindy looked doubtful, but Geoff went on. 'We are here because of events way back at the very beginning of the universe. Scientists tell us that before any order was put into the universe everything in the entire universe was compressed into a single point – they call it the "singularity". In the first infinitesimal fraction of a second in the life of the universe certain things like the speed at which the universe expanded, the strength of gravity and the power of the force between electric charges had to be fixed exactly right. If there hadn't been this "fine tuning", the universe would never have evolved as it has and life wouldn't have been possible. Doesn't this suggest that there was a Creator behind it all? Those who think that it does call the argument the 'anthropic principle'. Conditions had to be exactly right at the very beginning of the life of the universe for us to be here now.

Tim was a little doubtful about the value of this. 'So we need a God to set things in order at the beginning, and then he can just let it run on its own. Is that it?' he said. 'How then about the kind of God we are being asked to believe in? A God who just starts the universe off doesn't seem to be the kind of God we decided we wanted to believe in.'

Cindy remained unconvinced for a different reason. 'Perhaps scientists will one day discover why gravity and electricity and the expansion of the universe had to be as they are without dragging in a Creator to fix them exactly right. And anyway, how do we know that there aren't millions of universes and ours just arose by chance. We can't test how probable it is that our universe appeared.'

Anne was beginning to feel that all this was a bit beyond her. She appealed to Geoff. 'What does it all add up to?' she asked.

'Don't look at me as if I were the oracle', he laughed. 'Isn't it something like this? Evolution has shattered the idea that the natural world was deliberately designed by an intelligent Being. Recent research has shown that conditions had to be just right in the first moments of the expansion of the universe, but that doesn't prove conclusively that an intelligent Being set up those conditions. And in any case, as Tim pointed out, a God who simply set the universe going is hardly a God that we could call Father in the Christian sense. So, if you don't believe in God, these arguments aren't going to make you change your mind.

'On the other hand,' he went on, 'if you do believe in God, the fact that the universe exists and is marked by order and isn't chaos will be likely to confirm your faith.'

Anne was still not satisfied. 'I still think,' she said, 'that it is strange that the universe exists when it might not have done.'

'What do you mean?' said Tim.

'Well, all of us, I imagine, have wondered at some time or another, why there is a universe and not just nothing. Isn't it mysterious? Doesn't it suggest that God made it?'

Cindy didn't find this at all convincing. 'I don't see why you need to invent a God to explain the universe. It's just here, and we simply have to accept it. We can't even begin to suggest why it should exist.'

Anne found this very difficult to accept. She explained that she thought that it made much more sense to believe that behind the universe there is a God with an intelligent mind who made it than that it is just 'there'.

'But I can't see what it means to say that God "made" the universe,' Cindy replied. 'I know what it means for a carpenter to make a chair, or for a builder to build a house. They are part of the world and they are using the materials that are in the world to make the chair or house. But what can it mean to say that God "made" the universe? The building bricks of the universe weren't there for him to use. And what can it mean to talk about God "making" things before space and time existed?'

Geoff saw that Anne was looking rather dismayed, and he said, 'I think what Anne means is that the universe is so mysterious and wonderful that it is more difficult to believe that it just exists for no reason at all than to believe that there is a God behind it. But,' he went on, 'would such a suggestion convince anyone who doesn't believe in God already? I think Cindy is right when she says that there is such a vast difference between a carpenter making a chair and God making the universe that it is difficult to know what it can mean to say that God "made" the world.' You remember we were talking about "analogy" some time ago. To the unbeliever, the "analogy" between a man making a watch, or a carpenter making a chair, and God "making" the universe isn't close enough for the argument to stand up. But that doesn't mean that it makes no sense to the believer. Perhaps if we avoid using the word "made" or "created" and think simply that God is responsible for the world it would help.'

At this point Tim chipped in. 'I once heard someone say that God's creating the world was like a composer creating a symphony. Before he wrote the symphony it didn't exist. He created it out of nothing. Isn't that a closer analogy? Doesn't that help?'

Cindy shook her head, and Geoff said, 'I'm afraid it doesn't, Tim. Although the symphony as a symphony didn't exist until the composer wrote it, he was using sounds and instruments and violinists and flautists and trumpeters that do. You could just as well say that a chair didn't exist before the carpenter made it, especially if is was a new and unique design. Both the composer and the carpenter are part of the world – and God is not.'

They seemed to have talked themselves to a standstill. 'Where do we go from here?' Anne asked. They all looked at Geoff. 'Well, if you want me to suggest a topic,' he said, 'I suggest we try to discover why we believe in God.'

Questions for discussion

1. What do you make of the argument that the universe is like a watch and so requires a watchmaker?

2. Why did Geoff say that the analogy of a composer creating a symphony was no better than the analogy of the watchmaker?

3. If you have to believe in God before you can accept the arguments for his existence, what is their value or use?

7

Why Do We Believe in God?

Since Geoff had made the suggestion for the topic this week they waited for him to begin. 'We all know why Cindy doesn't believe in God,' he said. 'She has looked at the arguments for the existence of God and finds them all unconvincing. But I think that the rest of us found those that we looked at last week and the week before pretty unconvincing too. So why is she an atheist and the other three of us call ourselves Christians?' He looked across at Anne.

Anne was still worried. When Cindy had asked her why she believed in God, she couldn't give an answer, and none of the discussions they had had since had helped her to answer that question any better. So she said, 'When Cindy asked me that question, I admitted that I didn't know why I believed in God and I still don't. The arguments that we have talked about don't seem very convincing now, even though the universe seems mysterious to me and I wonder why there is something there rather than nothing at all. But I can see that it might just have happened by chance, as Cindy said.' She paused, and then added, 'I'll be honest. It seems to me that I believe in God – or perhaps I used to believe in God, because I'm getting a bit doubtful now – because I was brought up in a Christian home and it never occurred to me to doubt God's existence. My mother and father had a firm faith in God. I suppose they did think of him rather as the "old man in the sky", though I'm sure that they would have denied it if you'd put it just like that and would have talked about God being spirit.'

'Do you mean,' Cindy interrupted, 'that you never took the trouble to ask why you believed in God and whether he even existed?'

'I suppose that's right,' Anne admitted. 'But I'm not ashamed of it,' she added quickly. 'You see my parents were the most wonderful people I've ever known, and if believing in God was

31

the reason why they were so wonderful, that seems to me to be a worth-while reason for believing in God.'

By now Cindy had come to appreciate Anne's character sufficiently not to express the objections to this that she felt. Tim then said that he supposed that he'd come to believe in God because of the people he'd met in church. 'When everyone believes, it is natural that you should do the same,' he said.

At this point Geoff broke in. 'But then you met Cindy and stopped coming to church regularly, and began to have doubts. Is that right?' 'Cindy didn't stop me coming to church,' Tim retorted. 'We agreed that she would raise no objections to my odd little ways, so long as I didn't try to convert her. She came to church with me once, as you know, and she was so obviously uncomfortable that I vowed I would never ask her to come again. No, you can't blame Cindy. It's just that once I stopped coming to church regularly, believing in God seemed strange.'

Geoff wasn't going to let him get away with this quite so easily. 'So what you're saying is that you believed in God simply because the other people you were spending a lot of time with believed. Doesn't that mean that belief is simply accepting the ideas that you think your friends hold?' When Tim agreed that he supposed it was, Geoff went on, 'So belief in God is just a matter of belonging to a group where you were happy?'

'Not at all,' Tim responded, rather heatedly. 'We all did believe in God – really, really.' But Geoff was not going to be put off. 'I don't question that you all *thought* you were believing in God', he said, 'but what I'm saying is that your belief depended completely upon that group of people you met at church. Once you made a break with them you found that your faith was broken too.' Seeing that Tim was still looking very uncomfortable and perhaps a little upset, he added, 'I'm not saying your weren't sincere, or that you didn't *really* believe. What I am saying is that the *reason* why you believed in God was because you belonged to that church group. Some people might put it to you that your God was really the believing group. I wouldn't say that. But the answer to the question, "*Why* did you believe in God?" seems to me to be because you were a member of that church group.'

Cindy was listening to this interchange with some amusement. Now she joined in. 'So, Geoff, I suppose you'll say that the reason why I don't believe is because I didn't belong to a church group and my parents were not religious. I deny that. I looked at religion when I was in the sixth form and I didn't find any of the arguments for the existence of God at all convincing. And there's one other thing. We did some church history, and I was appalled at the way Christians behaved in the past. I came to see that religion is often evil and often increases the evil in the world. Religion seems to me not only to be unreasonable but also often to be malign.'

Anne felt that they were getting off the point, but Geoff seemed to want to pursue the subject a bit further. 'If I'm right,' he said, 'the three of us who call ourselves Christians came to our beliefs (and our doubts) mainly because of the people we mixed with. I did as well, and I can't see anything wrong in that. If we admire our parents and if we have good friends that is a good reason for trying to be like them. Our faith came from them. But now that we recognize it, we ought to go on to see whether our beliefs are justified. After all, all the church people may be deceiving themselves and their prayers may be no more than speaking to nothing. So I think we ought to distinguish between *why* we believe and whether our belief is *true*.' And then he added, with that grin that Anne found so appealing, 'Perhaps church people try to believe because they think all the other people in their church group believe more than they actually do!'

'What I find interesting,' Anne said, 'is why some people lose their faith. I mean people like that Church of England priest that Cindy told us about. Can you tell us any more about him, Cindy? I should like to know why he still thinks he can be a priest when he is obviously an atheist.'

'Well,' said Cindy, 'he described his loss of faith as a "conversion". Funny, isn't it. Most people talk of conversion *to* a religion. He spoke of having the courage to say that he didn't believe in God as a conversion to a genuine Christian faith. He doubted in fact whether he had ever really *believed* in God. Rather he had thought of God as a working hypothesis and, when the arguments for the existence of God no longer convinced him, he adopted a different working hypothesis – that a traditional God doesn't exist. But he still uses the word "God" for all his values and ideals put together.'

'I still think he is an atheist,' said Tim. 'And although I don't know the whole story, I think he lost his faith when he began to think about it. I wonder whether it's dangerous for us to be thinking about our faith now.'

'Oh Tim,' said Anne, 'you can't really mean that it's better to go on believing in God without trying to think it through. If I'm going to believe, I want it to be a belief that I adopt with my eyes open, not just because my parents were Christians. I may have accepted Christianity because of them at first, but now I want to think it out – even if I end up doubting God's existence.'

'Good for you,' said Cindy. 'You've almost persuaded me that I ought to become a Christian!' They all laughed.

'We don't seem to have got very much further tonight,' Tim said. 'Where do we go from here?'

'I've got an idea,' said Geoff. Suppose for next week we ask Cindy to tell us why she doesn't believe in God. So far we have simply looked at some of the arguments that have been put forward *for* belief. It might be interesting to look at the other side.'

Questions for discussion

1. What part do you think your friendship with other church people has played in your belief in God?

2. What do you think the priest meant by saying that once he had thought of God as a working hypothesis, but now his working hypothesis is that there *isn't* a God?

3. Geoff made a distinction between *why* we believe in God and whether that belief is *true*. Look at your own beliefs in the light of this distinction.

8

Cindy Explains Why She Became An Atheist

Cindy had been thinking about it all the week, and she was far from happy. The trouble was that she had found it easy to knock down the stock arguments for the existence of God, but it was quite another matter when she came to defend her atheism. It seemed to her, when she thought about it, that it was largely emotional. She had talked it over with Tim, and he'd encouraged her to tell her story to Anne and Geoff exactly as she'd told it to him. 'You've come to know them,' he said. 'They'll understand.'

When Cindy and Tim arrived, Anne saw immediately that Cindy was anxious and tried to put her at ease. 'You don't have to tell us why you don't believe in God if you don't want to,' she told her. 'We can easily discuss something else.' But Cindy said she wanted to. It would be the first time she'd talked about it to anyone apart from Tim, and she needed to bring it into the open. And she thought it would help them all to think about God.

When they were all comfortably settled and were drinking their coffee, Geoff asked Cindy if she would start them off. She began very diffidently. 'I suppose I never really believed in God, but you know how it is. In primary school the teachers act as if they all believed and I felt a bit odd. But I knew that neither my mother nor my father had much time for religion. We never went to church and they never talked about religion – although once, when we were driving past a convent surrounded by a high wall, Daddy said that that was religion gone mad.

'The crisis came when I was in the secondary school. Two things happened at about the same time. I was learning to play the cello, and had passed the first five grades of the music exams. You could play in the school orchestra when you had passed grade six, and I wanted to do that more than anything. I practised hard and felt certain I would do well. Daddy was a fine pianist and he always accompanied me in the exams. So we set off in great spirits, though I was a bit nervous, of course. Oh, it was awful.' She stopped, breathed hard, and then went on: 'Daddy started playing the introduction to the first piece, but it was all wrong. I couldn't make out the time, and there were so many wrong notes. I tried to start, but it just wouldn't go right. And then Daddy flew into a temper. I'd never known him angry before. Ever. He wasn't that kind of man. It was frightening. And that was the end of it. We went home in silence, and I burst into tears. It was that evening that Mummy told me that she was sure Daddy was ill, but he wouldn't go to the doctor. He had to go the next week because he crashed the car. After that he got worse very quickly. It was terrible. He was no longer the intelligent, witty, kind father, with a great sense of fun, that I knew. He couldn't feed himself. He could hardly say anything. He grew morose and sullen. Mummy looked after him, and she grew tired and cross and tearful. And then he died. I decided that if there was a God, he must be an absolute fiend to destroy Daddy like that.

'It was while all this was happening that we came to evolution in biology. One of the girls asked the teacher how she could believe in God if evolution was true, and she said she didn't. I suppose it was the first time I'd ever heard an adult admit that they didn't believe there was a God. Curiously I found it easier to accept Daddy's illness if there wasn't a God, so I became an atheist too. And reading those books by philosophers just confirmed it.'

The atmosphere had become a bit tense because they all felt so deeply for Cindy, but she added, 'That's it. Thank you so much for listening to me. I needed to say all that. I suppose it's just emotion really, but I've bottled it up for years and now it's come out I feel much better.'

They were all silent for a long time. At last Geoff spoke. 'I think you were wrong to say it's just emotion. I think that the evil and suffering in the world pose the most serious argument against the existence of God. Several of us spent a long time last year trying to understand how God could allow so much suffering if he really is good and really is in control of the world. And I don't think we came to any answer that fully satisfied us.'[1]

Cindy was a bit surprised that they'd found suffering a problem. She'd thought that Christians found a way round all the difficulties. If it was caused by human beings, they said it was because of the Fall. If it was illness or some other kind of disaster, they said it was divine punishment. Or they believed that God protected Christians who really believed. And if their prayers weren't answered, they said that God had given the answer 'no' because he had a better plan for them, or because they didn't have enough faith. To her it all seemed like a cop-out. You could find an explanation whatever happened.

Anne was pleased she had said that. It was exactly what she felt sometimes when she listened to some of the members at her church. She told Cindy that she found the problem of evil very difficult, but she was quite unable to accept the easy way out. She didn't believe that God sent suffering as punishment. She didn't believe that God gave special protection to Christians. She thought that the most difficult thing about evolution was the vast amount of suffering that it involved. And it was so wasteful – all those millions of creatures that were just thrown on the scrap-heap. And she wasn't going to accept any easy answers that made it impossible to present any counter evidence against belief in God. Then, more quietly, she added: 'I think it all comes back to Geoff's question, "What kind of God do we believe in?".'

Again they were all silent for quite a long time. Then Tim said, 'I suppose my idea of God was too simple. I'd never met

---

[1]   The account of their discussions is found in No. 5 in this series, *Why Evil and Suffering?* (Epworth Press, 1998).

any real suffering until I started to go out with Cindy and I gradually learnt what she's had to put up with. I told you the other week that it wasn't going out with Cindy that had made me doubt my faith, but I suppose it was, in a way. It wasn't that she argued me into not coming to church. We'd agreed to differ about religion. But what happened to her father made me think about God for the first time – seriously, I mean. I'd been a bit like those people that Cindy described, who could find a quick answer to everything. If you prayed for someone who was sick and they got better, that was an answer to prayer. If they died, that also was an answer. Either it showed that you didn't really have faith that God would heal your loved one, or God had given the answer "no". Just as she said. I suppose I thought of God very much as a human being – more powerful, of course, and kinder, but reacting to us in very human ways. Wasn't there a book published a long time ago with the title *Your God Is Too Small*? I think my God was too small. But what kind of a God would a greater one be?'

It was getting late – these conversations seemed to go on well into the night – and so they decided that they would think about Tim's question and discuss it next week.

Questions for discussion

1. What is your reaction to Cindy's account of her father's illness?

2. Geoff said that suffering presented the most serious question to the existence of God. What is the most serious problem for you?

3. How do you react to Tim's assertion that he had had too simple an idea of God?

9

Blind Faith?

When they next met Tim told the others that he'd been worrying about 'Your God is too small' all the week. What did it mean to say that God was 'small'? What kind of a God would a 'big' God be? 'We all agreed,' he said, 'that we didn't think of God as "an old man in the sky"' – but when he thought about the Old Testament that seemed to be exactly what the God of the Bible was. He was powerful all right. He could make a path through the sea for the Israelites to cross over and escape from Egypt, he could destroy Jericho and give victory to Israel's armies, he could even make the sun stand still, but he was no more than a tribal God, looking after the Israelites (and even punishing them sometimes), and having little concern or pity for the Canaanites or the Philistines. So although he was powerful, he was still a 'small' God.

Anne reminded them about Stephen. Stephen was no longer a member of their church – he'd decided that they were not 'real' Christians and had joined a thriving fundamentalist church – but just before he left he'd told them that one day he was driving up the motorway to an important Christian meeting where he was one of the speakers and suddenly noticed that his petrol tank was empty. There were no service stations on that motorway and the next intersection was nearly forty miles away. So he offered a prayer to God, and God had kept the engine going until he could get to his meeting. 'I think Stephen's God is not only small but also immoral,' she said. 'If he could keep Stephen's car going without any petrol, why didn't he do something about saving the millions of Jews that the Nazis killed – or prevent that earthquake in India?'

'So what kind of a God do you want to believe in?' Geoff asked. Anne wasn't sure. She thought of Fred. It seemed to her that for Fred, God was really Jesus. He was never tired of speaking about his 'Lord', and he did it in such an unselfconscious way that you never felt embarrassed. She'd never known anyone who could talk about Jesus so naturally – Fred spoke of Jesus as you might speak about any of your friends. 'Fred's God isn't powerful at all, at least not in the ordinary way. He's a sympathetic, caring, loving God, who is more willing to suffer himself than to punish any human being. Yet he isn't "soft". Fred is deeply upset by any wrongdoing because of the suffering it causes to Jesus. And it seems to me that the proof of his God lies in his own beautiful character.'

But Geoff pressed his question: 'But how about you?' Anne wasn't sure. She felt that Fred was the best Christian she was ever likely to meet, but even so, she wondered whether his idea of God was big enough to answer the questions of the scientists. 'Perhaps,' she said, 'we can only think about what God is *not*. I mean, he isn't limited by time or space. He is immortal. He is everywhere. No, that isn't right. He is outside of time and space, because he existed before there was any universe. He isn't part of the world, he's outside it in some way. Oh, I don't know. He's "spiritual" I suppose, though I'm not sure what that means. But he must be "personal" in some way, because we couldn't worship mere impersonal power could we?' She stopped.

All this time Cindy had been listening with some amusement. Now at last she joined in. 'But if all that you can say about God is what he is *not*, how is that different from there being no God at all?' Anne looked even more puzzled, so Cindy went on: 'Your friend Stephen's God did at least *do* something, but it seems to me that your God doesn't do anything at all. What difference would it make if he didn't exist? None, as far as I can see.'

'That's a good point,' said Geoff. 'A philosopher once made up a little parable. He said that two explorers came upon a clearing in a forest where there was a garden, with plants and many weeds. One of them said that a gardener had made it, but the other thought it just happened by chance. They kept watch, but no gardener ever came. They got some blood hounds (how

41

they managed to get them in the middle of the jungle, I don't know!) but the dogs never barked. "There you are," said the sceptical explorer, "I told you there wasn't any gardener." But the other explorer still wasn't convinced. "There *is* a gardener," he said, "it's just that we can't see him."'

Anne and Tim were both intrigued by this. 'What you are saying,' said Tim, 'is that we can define God in such a way that it is impossible to deny that he exists, but if we do that there's nothing left to show us that he does.' Geoff was pleased that he'd seen the point. 'Well, then,' Tim went on, 'if you agree with Anne that God is so great that we cannot even imagine what he is like, and that he doesn't do anything special – he doesn't perform "miracles" – so that we can say emphatically, "*that* is the work of God", why do you believe in God? Or are you like that Anglican priest that Anne is so interested in?'

'I didn't say that I agreed with the philosopher,' Geoff answered. 'Indeed, I think that if you start from where he is, there's no way of proving that God exists. What I am saying is that one of the important things about God that we ought to take into account is the way he communicates with human beings and the way he cares for them.'

'I'm on the side of the philosopher,' said Cindy. 'Explain what you mean.'

'It's like this,' Geoff began. 'If you demand as proof of God's existence examples of things that he's actually *doing* you will never be satisfied, because an alternative explanation can always be given. Stephen's car had a faulty fuel gauge. That person you prayed for would have got better in any case. Or perhaps it was psychosomatic – the fact that the people in her church were praying for her gave her the confidence to overcome the disease. And as we saw the other week, the evil and suffering in the world is a very strong counter-argument against the existence of a good and loving God. You may be able to explain away some of the suffering – that terrorist bomb in Omagh was placed there by evil men; the hundreds of people who have died in India need not have died because their houses should have been built more strongly in an area where there were frequent earthquakes. No, it's the whole evil of the evolution of the universe that is the trouble.'

'So what you are saying,' said Cindy, 'is that it's just a matter of blind faith. You believe in God, I don't, but the evidence that we both look at is exactly the same.' She paused, and then she said, 'It's funny how things we read at school keep coming into my mind. There was a marvellous poem by Robert Browning in which a sceptical bishop tries to defend his doubts. At one point he suggests that the world is like a chess board:

> All we have gained then by our unbelief
> Is a life of doubt diversified by faith,
> For one of faith diversified by doubt:
> We called the chess-board white, – we call it black.

'I think that's right,' said Geoff. 'There can be no real faith that isn't mixed up with doubt. In the end, I believe that you simply have to take your stand on goodness, truth, and beauty. And I can quote poetry as well! Studdert Kennedy experienced the darkest side of life in the trenches during the first world war, and in one of his poems he says:

> How do I know that God is good? I don't.
> I gamble like a man. I bet my life
> Upon one side in life's great war. I must,
> I can't stand out. I must take sides.

And he ends up with some words that I have always kept in my inner heart as a kind of anchor for my own faith:

> You want to argue? Well,
> I can't. It is a choice. I choose the Christ.

It doesn't mean that I'm not willing to discuss religion. I enjoy it. But in the end I'm convinced that there is no certainty either way. As Studdert Kennedy said, "It is a choice".'

'So you're no different from that Anglican priest,' retorted Cindy, 'only he was honest about it. He admitted that he didn't believe that God exists, and then he tried to work out what the basis of his life was to be. But both you and Anne are simply siding with things like goodness, and trying to say at the same time that there is a God. But you admit that there's no proof at all. It seems to me that you're all atheists at heart.

'One thing troubles me, though. If there is no God, and if this life is all that there is, what is the value of goodness and all the human virtues? In the end both good and evil will cease to exist and all human endeavour will be destroyed. Whether the universe ends in the 'big crunch' or a cold silence, in the end there won't be anyone to mourn its passing.'

'I think there is an answer to that,' Geoff replied, but we shall have to leave it until next week, shan't we?'

Questions for discussion

1. Tim said that the God of the Old Testament was just a tribal God. What do you think?

2. What is your response to Anne's assertion that all we can say about God is what he is *not*?

3. How would you describe faith? Is it just a blind step into the dark?

10

Is God Needed To Sustain Morality?

They had all been thinking hard about Cindy's comment. It seemed all right just to be arguing about whether God exists and what kind of a God he might be, but when it came down to the value of goodness and whether goodness had any real existence it was a different matter. So they were all eager to start the discussion when they met together at Anne's home. The trouble was that Anne and Tim didn't know where to begin, and Geoff was obviously not going to tell them what he thought straight away. Just like him!

After each one of them had tried to express their ideas, and come to a stop, Geoff turned to Cindy. 'You said that if there is no God, then whether the universe ends in the 'big crunch' or in a cold silence makes no difference. In the end there is no difference between good and evil, and we might as well all live utterly selfish lives.'

'I didn't say that,' Cindy replied. 'The point I was wanting to make was that it is quite illogical to doubt whether God exists and yet believe that goodness and truth are somehow "eternal".'

Anne felt, however, that Cindy's own position was just as illogical. After all, she declared that she was an atheist, and now she said that everything that was good and beautiful would one day come to an end, yet this did not stop her being the kind and happy person that she was. 'So why do you think that it is important to be moral?' she asked.

'At the very least,' Cindy replied, 'morality oils the wheels of society. Just think what it would be like if everyone told lies all the time, and never kept promises, and never helped anyone else. What kind of life would it be if you never knew who you could trust, and whenever you met anyone you had to try to kill them first or they would probably kill you?'

'That's going a bit far,' said Tim. 'There's honour even among thieves.'

'But that just proves my point,' said Cindy. 'Every society needs the oil. And everyone knows that it needs it, so everyone applies the oil can within their own little group. Only with criminals it's just that their group doesn't include their victims.'

They began to feel that they weren't getting very far, and Anne turned to Geoff. 'Come on,' she said, 'you can't leave us all in suspense any longer. You said last week that there was an answer to the final futility of the universe. What is it?'

Geoff still seemed very hesitant. Then he said, 'I know Cindy will say it's all nonsense and is no more a valid argument for the existence of God than those other "proofs" that we all agreed were pretty feeble. But there was once a great philosopher. He was very doubtful whether you could prove God's existence, but he said that two things presented him with a sense of wonder: "the starry skies above and the moral law within". I suppose what he meant was something like this. He felt a sense of wonder as he looked at the stars, and that sense of wonder was in a kind of way, belief in God.

'But even more, he felt he had a duty to do what is right. For him "what is right" couldn't be simply what he chose to regard as right. It wasn't that he believed that duty was what God commanded. He would have rejected that vehemently. You had to decide for yourself where your duty lay, he asserted. Just to do what someone else told you wasn't true goodness. Yet somehow goodness was so important to him that it made him wonder whether there wasn't a God to secure that it was eternal.'

Cindy wasn't convinced. 'You seem to want some kind of absolute "goodness" that exists up there in the sky. But as far as I can see that's nonsense. When a man throws himself into the raging sea to try to save a child he has never met before, the only goodness that exists lies in what he does. There isn't

46

something that we can call "courage"' or "self-sacrifice" somewhere "up there". And it doesn't need a God to make it real.'

'That isn't what I meant,' Geoff said. 'I agree with you that there are no such things as "goodness" or "bravery" in the abstract. But take your example of the man sacrificing his life for a strange child. Unless there is a God to give him life after death, that man's goodness died with him.'

Cindy wasn't convinced. 'Even if our goodness dies with us, goodness is still better than evil. I know that in my bones. Everyone knows it – except a few psychopaths. I don't need a God to make goodness good, and I certainly don't think that the fact that we value goodness so highly proves that there is a God who will take good people to heaven.'

'Aren't you mixing up two things, Cindy?' said Geoff. 'I agree with you that you don't need a God to make goodness good, but doesn't the fact that we all agree that goodness is so important suggest that we are conscious of a world beyond this one? Or put it another way, the fact that we have a sense of the importance of duty and right and goodness takes us out of a purely material existence of being born, eating, sleeping, breeding and dying into what I would call "the spiritual", and that is close to believing in God.'

'How vulgar you are,' said Tim. '"eating, sleeping and breeding"! It makes us sound like animals.' 'That's just my point,' Geoff responded. 'We can be described as just like animals. Yet we know that we are more than that. Part of that "more" is our belief in the importance of goodness. And that makes us think of supreme goodness, which is pretty close to saying that we believe in God.'

Cindy was still doubtful. 'I agree that to say that it is necessary to have a God to establish what is right and what is wrong is one thing, and to argue from our sense of good and evil to the existence of God is another, but neither claim, it seems to me, is true. I don't think there are any objective

47

values. And I do not believe that goodness lasts any longer than the life of the person who does good. This life is all there is. And we make goodness and evil for ourselves.'

Anne felt she was getting a bit out of her depth. 'What do you mean by values being "objective"?' she asked. 'Look at it like this,' said Cindy. 'Tim tells me that many of the people in church were horrified when they discovered that two of their church members started living together when they weren't married. Several people said they should be told they couldn't belong to their church any more. I don't know them, but I suppose they love one another and both think that that is all that matters. That shows that there's no universal rule about sex and marriage. Those two think one thing, the other church people think something else. And there are very many things just like that. Think about war and pacifism, or whether animals should be used in medical research. So there is no absolute standard.'

'But there are some things that everyone agrees are wrong', Anne retorted. 'Everyone, surely, believes that murder is wrong, even if there are plenty who can see nothing wrong about adultery.' Cindy wouldn't have this either. 'It's all a matter of what you call murder. Murder isn't just killing a human being. When a soldier kills an enemy he's commended, not blamed.'

Geoff intervened. 'I think the two of you are still mixing things up,' he said. 'The fact that people don't agree about what is right and what is wrong doesn't of itself mean that there is no absolute standard of right and wrong. It may just be that we haven't found it yet. Or maybe it depends on the situation. It may be that killing is wrong in almost all circumstances, but if there is no other way to protect a child, to risk killing the attacker would be right.

'On the other hand, the fact that we believe so strongly in goodness shows that we are more than animals, and that may point to the existence of a God.

48

'But I'm not saying that right is right because God says it is so. Some people have argued that every moral law requires a lawgiver, and this lawgiver must be God. I don't accept that at all. For one thing, goodness is not a moral law. And even if it is thought of as a law, that doesn't mean that someone gave the command.'

This carried no weight with Cindy, and even the other two felt that Geoff's passionate devotion to goodness perhaps led him to go beyond what could be proved. They seemed to have reached an end of any useful discussion, so they decided to call it a day. 'Where do we go from here?' asked Anne. 'I assume you still want to come round to my place next week.' They couldn't think of a topic and decided to see what thoughts came to them during the week.

Questions for discussion

1. Why do you think it is important to be moral?

2. Consider whether there are any absolute standards of right and wrong?

3. Geoff said that our conviction of the value of goodness suggests that there is a God. What do you make of this argument?

11

A Novel Suggestion

When they met at Geoff's they wondered what was left to discuss, but Geoff had a surprise for them.

'How do you know that Tim has a mind?' he asked Anne. She was so taken aback she didn't know what to say. In the end she blurted out. 'Of course he has a mind. We all have.'

'But how do you *know*?' Geoff persisted. 'All you can see and touch is his body. You hear him speak. You watch what he does. But how do you *know* he isn't just a superior kind of robot?'

Anne felt that this was absurd. 'I'm a person, not just a "superior kind of robot", she answered. 'And since we are all human beings I just know that Tim is a person. I've got a mind He's got a mind. We're both persons. We both have minds.'

But Geoff kept at it. 'He's got a brain – at least we could take a brain scan to make sure, and if he died we could carry out a post mortem and cut out his brain and weigh it. But that doesn't show that he has a mind.'

Tim began to feel slightly embarrassed and Cindy felt sorry for Anne. 'Geoff, give Anne a break,' she said. 'We all know that you can't prove that we've got minds if you stick to what can be weighed and measured. We just know we have.' Tim added, 'What's all this to do with believing in God anyway?'

'That's just my point,' said Geoff. 'You can't prove that Tim has a mind, but you are quite confident that he has. Nothing is likely to shake your belief. Isn't that exactly like our position with God? We have seen that we can't prove that God exists. But if we believe that other people have minds, why not believe that God exists?'

'I think that's just about the silliest argument I've ever heard,' said Cindy. 'Believing that Tim has a mind is completely different from believing in God. For one thing, as Anne said, we're all human beings, so that we know from inside that we

50

have minds. For another, we can see Tim, watch what he does, hear what he says. God is invisible, so we don't know if he's there at all. No sane person doubts that other people have minds. It would be quite irrational to suppose that people are just bodies. We should call anyone who thought that people were just superior robots insane.'

'You don't see my point,' said Geoff. 'What I'm suggesting is that it is just as rational to believe in God as to believe in other minds. We were talking the other week about "sheer belief" as if this were something quite irrational, for which we couldn't give any reasons. What I'm suggesting is that it is no less rational than believing that Tim has a mind.'

They were all silent for some minutes. At last Anne said, 'I really can't see that. We can see Tim and catch hold of him. We can ask him questions and he answers us. We know what he thinks because he tells us. And, as I said, he's one of us. We all have minds.'

'Everything you've said except the last would be true of the perfect computer', Geoff responded, 'and yet you are absolutely convinced that Tim has a mind. It you think it rational to believe that, isn't it just as rational to believe in God? You believe that Tim is a spiritual being because what he says and does reveals it. In the same way, we believe in God's existence because of the signs he has given us. The one is no more irrational than the other.'

'Hold on,' Cindy interposed. 'You said we believe in God's existence because of the signs he has given us. What "signs"?'

'Well,' said Geoff, 'in the first place there is religious experience.'

'But we dismissed that the first time we all met,' retorted Cindy. 'We agreed that it was sufficient proof for the person who had an experience that he or she interpreted as God, but it wouldn't stand up as an argument for anyone else.'

'I wonder whether we dismissed it too quickly,' Geoff replied. 'I think you and Anne were quite right to be sceptical

51

about it. Too many people have deceived themselves that they have met God, and some of the stories of people's religious experience are just plain daft. But even if you've never had a religious experience (and I don't think any of us has), some of the accounts of such experiences "ring true", and the way they have changed people's lives seems to support that. Think of Bishop Hugh Montefiore who saw Jesus when he was a boy at a public school, and it changed the whole of his life. He gave up Judaism and became a Christian. Now I don't think there is any reason to be more sceptical about that than to believe that Tim has a mind.'

But Cindy wasn't going to give up quite so easily. 'I still can't see why we should accept what people say about their experiences as being actual experiences of God. What they see is always moulded by the beliefs that they have already. Protestants and Muslims are not likely to have visions of the Virgin Mary, but Catholics will.'

Anne wasn't paying much attention. She was still thinking about what Geoff had said, and she turned to him. 'Does that mean, then, that religious experience is the most important proof of God's existence?' she asked.

'Not quite,' Geoff replied. My point is that just because none of the so-called "proofs" of God's existence provide a knock-down argument that will convince an atheist, there is no reason to be ashamed of our own belief in God. It is quite as reasonable as believing in other people's minds. Oh, I know it's rather a weak argument, but we shouldn't reject an argument just because it isn't perfect. A weak argument is different from a bad argument.'

'So what you are saying,' Tim said, 'is that there are only weak arguments for our belief that other people have minds and that there is a God, but that is no reason for rejecting either belief. Is that right?'

'Yes,' said Geoff. 'Oh, I know it sounds pretty feeble, but look at it like this. When we meet other people what we say and do assumes that they have minds. So what is wrong with living as if God exists? We can't know for certain. All we can do is to live as if our beliefs are true.'

'That sounds like that poem by Studdert Kennedy that you quoted to us the other week,' Tim said, but Cindy commented, 'It all sounds to me a bit like Pascal's wager, and I'm not sure that I can go along with that.' 'What's that?' Tim and Anne said together. But Geoff looked at the clock. 'I think we shall have to wait for that until next week,' he said.

Questions for discussion

1. What do you think of Geoff's argument that it is as rational to believe in God as it is to believe that other people have minds?

2. Geoff suggested that all we can do is to live as if our beliefs are true. But what if they are false after all?

3. What 'signs' of God's existence can you offer?

4. What do you make of Bishop Montefiore's experience of seeing Jesus while he was still a Jew?

12

Pascal's Wager

As soon as they were comfortably seated in the armchairs in her flat, Anne said to Cindy, 'Come on now, we're all dying to hear about Pascal's wager. I know he was a great mathematician, and wrote *Pensées* (though I've never read them), but what about his wager?'

'Pascal compared the choice between believing in God and being an atheist with a gambler's choice in a game of chance. He pointed out that what is rational depends not only on the probabilities (whether the coin will fall heads or tails), but the level of the stakes. In the choice of whether to believe that there is a God or not, the stakes are very high. If you believe in God and you are right you gain eternal happiness. But if you believe in God and you are wrong you lose nothing at all. Indeed, what you would gain is a virtuous life. So even if the probability of there being a God is not very high, it is entirely rational to stake everything on his existence.'

The others were silent for quite a long time, trying to take this in. Anne was the first to speak. 'I suppose that's all right if you're coldly logical. But how can anyone simply *decide* to believe? You can't possibly wake up one morning and say, "Right, from now on I believe in God." It doesn't seem to me that Pascal knew what faith is.'

Tim agreed with Anne, but went even further. 'It all seems pretty selfish to me. Do you want to be rewarded with eternal bliss? Well then, believe that God exists.'

'I don't think you have quite seen what Pascal was driving at,' Cindy said. 'He wasn't saying that you make up your mind to adopt an intellectual belief that God exists. He meant that you should order your whole life as if he did. For Pascal that meant going to Mass (he was a devout Catholic), but for us, I suppose, it would mean going to church each Sunday, praying each day (even when we feel that there is no one to hear our prayer), reading the Bible, and doing all the loving things that is expected of the Christian.'

Anne was still unhappy. 'But there still seems something phoney about the whole idea. I think we need to decide what faith really is. Even if you are right, faith is something more than going through the outward motions of religion.' She turned to Geoff. 'You've been silent as usual. What do you think about it?'

He spoke rather hesitantly. 'I think Pascal could only present his wager because he was already a Christian. It's just the same with Studdert Kennedy. They both were already believers, though Kennedy had to face up to doubt. So what the betting meant for both of them was living out the faith they had. Now that's fine, so long as the faith is a good faith. But what if the faith was that of a Satanist? Living out his or her faith would mean doing things which ordinary people would condemn as utterly evil. Or how about those sects that induced their adherents to commit mass suicide – or perhaps even murdered them?'

'So you think as I do,' Anne replied. 'Unless you can be sure that your belief is true, it is superstition – and it can become a dangerous superstition?'

'Yes,' said Geoff, 'and that's why I think it is so important that we think through our faith – even if that makes us less certain in the end.'

It seemed that they all agreed with this. But then Anne said: 'We may say that it is important to think through our faith, but does that simply mean trying to decide whether God exists or not?'

'What are you thinking of?' Cindy asked. Anne wasn't sure. She still couldn't get over her surprise at Geoff's suggestion that we should compare belief in the existence of other minds with belief in God, and she was worried about the relation between belief in God and morality. Had they worked through the implications of these questions properly? And she had a niggling feeling at the back of her mind that they had moved a long way from the beliefs of the people she knew in her church.

Fred would have been horrified by Pascal's wager, because he was so utterly devoted to his Lord. And while some of the other church members believed very strongly that what they called the modern immorality and evil in society was due to most people abandoning Christianity, Anne knew that some of her friends at work who were not Christians were kinder and less selfish than some of the people at church, and several of them did far more for disadvantaged people in society. So she was very glad when Tim asked, 'Where do we go from here?'

'Suppose we go back over the way we have come, and see if there is anything we have left out that's important,' Geoff suggested. They all agreed that this would be a good idea.

Questions for discussion

1. How would you define faith?

2. What is the difference between faith and superstition?

3. What differences can you see between Pascal's wager and Studdert Kennedy's bet on the Christ (see p. 41)?

13

Looking Back

When the friends met at Anne's they wondered whether it was going to be the last of their discussions. They had decided to look back over the last three months and try to see where they had got to, but weren't quite sure how to go about it. 'Would it be a good idea if we each explained what each of us has gained from our discussions and what difference they have made to us,' Anne suggested.

'I'll start,' said Cindy. 'Yes, I really want to, because I've learnt so much.'

She explained how angry she had been when Anne had presented herself on the doorstep that first time. She felt she had come to try to get Tim back to church, and probably try to convert her as well. But now she was sad that this looked as if it might be the last of their discussions. What had she learnt? So much that it was difficult to know where to start.

She had been surprised that people who went to church could be so open about their beliefs and their doubts. She had pictured church people very differently. She had, in fact, come to see that true faith cannot be separated from doubt, so that in a funny sort of way she had drawn closer to belief. No, that wasn't quite what she meant. At least she wasn't as fixed in her atheism. She had learnt that religious belief need not be *unreasonable*, and that her atheism was a *belief* just as much as belief in God was.

She was going to go on, but Geoff stopped her. 'Before you convert Anne and Tim,' he said with a grin, 'I'd like to hear what they made of it all.'

'I suppose I'd better make my confession,' Tim said. 'After all, if it hadn't been for me we should never had have these discussions at all.' He reminded them of the way various things had led him into stopping coming to church, and how only Anne seemed at all concerned. 'It's no wonder we lose church

57

members,' he said. 'If it had gone on for a few weeks more I don't think I should ever have come to church again.'

He recalled how God had seemed to fade out of his life after he had stopped coming, and how he had thought about him far more after Anne's visit than he had ever done before. So what he had once thought was faith in God had really been pleasure in joining in with the people he met in church.

He looked at Cindy and gave a rather shamefaced laugh. 'I suppose I largely went for the girls – and the boost doing all those things in church gave to my ego. When I met Cindy I didn't need those things.' But now, he explained, he had begun to realize the importance of thinking about God and about what religion is all about. 'I think I'm still mixed up, and I suppose I've come to doubt God almost as much as Cindy, but at least I've come to see that the main thing is to understand what kind of a God I'm believing in – or doubting. That for me is the most important thing that has come out of our discussions.'

'Well, Anne?' said Geoff.

Anne found it easy to start, but much more difficult to carry on. 'The thing that made the greatest impression upon me through the whole of our discussions,' she said, 'was that first question that Cindy asked me. "Why do you believe in God?" And I still don't know. I *do* believe, and that's largely because over the years Geoff has taught me to be relaxed about religion – not to be anxious about the authority of the Bible, to accept that there is no answer to the problem of evil and suffering that will fully satisfy us, that life after death is a mystery, indeed that in everything we have to trust in God and live with our doubts. I do believe, I do still pray, but I find greater help from silent worship than from boisterous hymns and mission songs.

'The arguments that try to prove God's existence didn't convince me any more than they convinced Cindy. I suppose I responded most readily to that poem by Studdert Kennedy about choosing the Christ. I can't see that there is any other way. But I sometimes wish I had the quiet, confident faith that

Fred has. He is my ideal of what a Christian ought to be. And I wish I could say I'd had an experience of God.'

Their eyes now turned to Geoff, who remained silent. At last Tim said, 'Come on Geoff, we've all bared our souls. The least you can do is to tell us what you believe.'

'All right,' he said at last, 'it's only fair, but you will probably have realized by now that I'm the perpetual observer. I like to look on, pick up this argument and that, turn it over, push it here and there, prod one or two of you, but never let you know what I think myself. I can always see three sides to every pound coin – and the milled edge is often the most intriguing. And over the years I've become less and less certain. I was quite clear about the Bible. I could think my way through the problem of evil, though with some difficulty. But life after death floored me. And that has made me almost paranoid about my faith. I simply *do not know*. At times I almost wish I could be an atheist. I'd have something clear-cut then. But I can't be. And I can't be an agnostic either. I suppose my patron saint is Studdert Kennedy.'

He stopped, and Anne was just going to suggest that they should have another cup of coffee, when he began again. 'I'm most grateful to you all. To Cindy for being so forthright and for showing me that you can't prove God's existence. I knew that, of course, but she made it so plain. To Tim for his honesty in looking at his motives. To Anne for just being Anne. So where do I stand?

'The most important thing, it seems to me, is to be clear about what kind of God we are believing in – or rejecting. I think that most people fail to do that, and so they never sort out their belief or their reasons for believing in God. Is he the Master Magician, or the Great Daddy, simply Jesus, or the God who can be spoken of only by saying what he is *not*? And is that priest a Christian when he says that he doesn't believe in a transcendent God, but still uses the word God for his highest ideals? But no one throughout all these weeks has mentioned

the Trinity, even though three of us are churchgoers (and I
include Tim!). I wonder why.

'Then I can't dismiss the arguments for the existence of God
as easily as you three do. Oh, I know that none of them is a
knock-down argument. If it were, I suppose, the only atheists
would be fools! But I find them helpful. With Anne I am
perplexed at the universe: why is there anything when there
might be nothing. The arguments don't *prove* that there is a
God, but if you trust that there is, they show that it isn't a
totally irrational belief. And I find that very important indeed.

'I'm very uncertain about religious experience. I've never had
any kind of religious experience at all. I've never seen Jesus as
our former minister says he did. I've never had that sense of
peace that Fred talks about. I'm such a cold fish that I always
feel something of a spectator during services. I don't doubt for
one moment that people have experiences. My trouble is the
same as Cindy's. I think it's all too easy to think a gush of
emotion is an experience of God. And the experiences which
people claim to have had can be explained away so easily. I
suppose that if I'd had a religious experience I should be
certain of God. But I haven't. I don't know why.

'So in the end, I suppose, I hope rather than believe. I practise
religion. I try to follow what I accept as the teaching of Jesus.
I'm absolutely certain of the importance of working for justice.
But in the end, like Anne, I'm a gambler – along with Studdert
Kennedy.'

He paused. 'Well, there you are,' he added, with his usual
grin. 'You've dragged things out of me that I've never told
anyone before.'

Again they were silent, and then Cindy said: 'I think we
should keep on meeting. None of us gets much out of church
services, it seems. I certainly found that service that Tim took
me to highly embarrassing – those hymns, that greeting each
other with the peace, that preacher. But all of us have got a

great deal out of our meeting together. Perhaps we could make them a little more "spiritual".'

She spoke for them all. But Anne added, rather tentatively, 'Do you think we could meet next week and discuss the Trinity? Geoff expressed surprise that we haven't mentioned it before.' So they agreed to do that.

Questions for discussion

1. Look back over the previous twelve chapters. What things that were said in them made most impression on you?

2. Why do you think Cindy suggested that they might make future meetings more 'spiritual'? What did she mean?

3. Tim seems to have ended up with a more fragile faith than he started with, while Cindy has come to understand what religion is all about a little better. What effect have their discussions had on you?

14
The Christian God

It was Anne who spoke first. 'Last week,' she said, 'Geoff asked why none of us had mentioned the Trinity. I've been thinking about that and the answer I've come up with is this. We didn't mention the Trinity because the God we've been talking about for most of the time isn't the Christian God.'

Tim looked astonished, and Cindy seemed a bit surprised. 'Go on,' Geoff said.

'Well,' Anne continued, 'it's like this. We agreed that that Anglican priest was an atheist. A real God must exist in his own right. You can't just have high ideals and call them God. We also agreed that God is not "an old man in the sky", or the "Master Magician". I think we weren't completely happy with Fred's God, although those who know him regard him as the finest Christian they've ever met. God is surely more than just Jesus. So in the end we all fastened on the God who can only be spoken of by saying what he is *not*. But that, surely, isn't the Christian God. Didn't someone once say, "God of Abraham, God of Isaac, God of Jacob, not the God of the philosophers"? Haven't we been talking simply about "the God of the philosophers"?'

'I'm not sure I understand what you're driving at,' said Tim. 'I thought we had agreed that a God who came down and spoke to people like Abraham wasn't the kind of God we could believe in. That is, unless you treat those stories in the Old Testament as visions. What other kind of God can you believe in today except the God of the philosophers?'

Cindy agreed with Tim. 'The reason why I was an atheist was that I thought that Christians believed in the Great Daddy God. Now I see that God can be thought of in a different way, in a way that makes sense to me. I'm still not convinced that he exists, but for me, if there is a God who exists he must be that kind of God. So I still have no patience with the ideas that I think many people who go to church have. At least,' she added, 'that's the picture of God that some of those speakers on the radio seem to have. A God who made human beings in his own image. A God who somehow controls history. A God who keeps on interfering in the events in the world.

'Oh, the man who said, "God of Abraham, God of Isaac, God of Jacob, not the God of philosophers or scholars" was Pascal again. He had a deeply moving spiritual experience that made such an impression on him that he wrote this saying down on a piece of parchment and sewed it into his clothes. It actually goes on with an ecstatic cry: "Certainty. Certainty. The heart! Joy. Peace".'

They all turned to Geoff. 'You mentioned the Trinity,' said Tim. 'What have you got to say about it?'

Geoff explained that the idea of the Trinity was an attempt to make sense of the experience of the first Christians, and what many Christians believe about God today. He pointed out that the first Christians were Jews, and that they had grown up to say every day, 'Hear, O Israel: The Lord our God, the Lord is one; and you shall love the Lord your God with all your heart, and with all your soul, and with all your might.' This was a declaration of devotion to the one God of Israel, the God who created the universe. As Jews they despised the Gentiles who worshipped many gods.

'But then they met Jesus, and they became convinced that he was more than simply a man. They believed that he had risen from the dead, and they began to pray to him. They called him the Son of God. That didn't mean that he was literally God's son, and they probably didn't think of him as divine in the same way that God the Father is, but they felt they had to worship him.

'Then they experienced a strange power which they called the Holy Spirit, and they came to think that the Spirit was also divine.'

'So now they believed in three Gods,' said Anne. 'No,' Geoff replied. 'A little later on, Christian thinkers tried to work out what it all meant. They certainly didn't believe that there were three Gods. And most of them didn't believe that the Father, Jesus, and the Holy Spirit were just three ways in which God revealed himself to them. And they didn't suppose that God was first of all the Creator, then became the Son, and is now the Spirit. So they said he is all three all the time, although he is still only one God.'

'Thanks for the theology lesson,' said Anne, 'but I still don't see how it can work out. I mean, don't most people that we know in church really believe in three Gods?' She saw that Tim was looking doubtful, so she went on: 'Take that baptism last Sunday. The minister poured three cupfuls of water over the head of that poor baby and said: "in the name of the Father – and of the Son – and of the Holy Spirit". If that isn't three Gods I don't know what is. Then there's "the grace". We separate out the grace of the Lord Jesus Christ, the love of God, and the fellowship of the Holy Spirit.'

Cindy joined in at last. 'I've read a book or two about the Trinity,' she said. 'As far as I can see, most of the writers begin with the dogma that God is a Trinity – three persons in one God – and then struggle to make some sort of sense of it. In the end most of them make him three Gods. They even point to that famous Russian icon which pictures the Trinity in such a way that it is the three Gods that stand out most prominently. Sometimes they emphasize the love the Father, the Son and the Spirit have between them. Doesn't that imply that they are three separate Gods.'

Tim felt that they ought to get back to the question of what difference it made to believe in the Trinity rather than the God of the philosophers. He turned to Geoff. 'What have you got to say about all this?'

'I confess that I'm puzzled,' Geoff answered. 'I suppose some people would call me a Unitarian. Perhaps we should think about Fred. We said on one occasion that God for Fred was just Jesus. I don't believe that's right, but I'm sure that many people in the church think like that. All those choruses about Jesus my Friend. Fred's different. He believes that God is *like* Jesus. For him Jesus is God's way of revealing himself to us. Jesus is his Lord. That was what I was thinking about when I wondered why we hadn't mentioned the Trinity.'

Now it was Anne's turn to be puzzled. 'Are you suggesting,' she said, 'that the final proof of the existence of God is that he revealed himself to us in Jesus?'

'Not exactly,' Geoff replied. 'I'm not saying that I believe that, because I find it difficult to think of Jesus as more than a human being. What I *am* saying is that you mustn't be led astray by an old heretic like me. The orthodox Christian faith is that Jesus is the Son of God and so God revealed himself to us through him. Jesus both proves that there is a God and shows us what he's like.'

Anne still had doubts. 'But everything then depends on what we think about Jesus. And we had some problems when we were thinking about the Bible.'

'I know,' Geoff answered, 'and perhaps we need to look again at the Gospels.[1] What I'm interested in, though, is what is the relation between "the God of the philosophers" and "the Father of our Lord Jesus Christ". It seems to me that before you can believe that Jesus revealed God you have to believe that God exists, and that is a matter for the philosophers.'

Questions for discussion

1. Anne said that the God that the four friends had been talking about wasn't the Christian God. What do you make of this assertion?
2. Say over the grace to yourself. What picture of God does it put in your mind?

---

[1] See the volume about Jesus to be published later in this series.

3. What is the relation between the Christian God and 'the God of the philosophers'?

Part 2

Thinking Through The Issues

15

What Kind of a God?

When Cindy asked Anne why she believed in God, Anne found it difficult to give an answer, because she had never thought about the question before. In this book we may well be thinking about questions that have never occurred to you or that you've never been asked. People sometimes say that this shows that it is better to retain a 'simple faith' and not to venture into critical discussions. Indeed, sometimes young people have been advised by sincere church members not to take theological courses in colleges and universities because they will destroy their faith. But the questions will not go away, however much we may shut our eyes to them. 'Why do you believe in God?' is a perfectly fair question to put to any Christian.

Geoff's question in chapter 3 also floored Anne: 'What do you mean by "God"?' She had taken it for granted that everyone knows what 'God' means. It was only when Geoff pressed her to say what she understood by the word that she was pushed into thinking about a name that she had used all her life without bothering to think about its precise meaning. She found that it was far from easy to say exactly what her idea of God was.

These two questions lie at the heart of our discussions in this book, and they are closely related. To ask why you believe in God makes no sense if you have only a hazy idea of what you believe in, and whether you are to be counted a believer or not depends on what idea you have about God. This is probably why so many people answer opinion polls that they believe in God. Hardly ever are they asked what they mean by God. Yet you cannot be an atheist without knowing what kind of a God it is you do *not* believe in!

Perhaps, then, the most important thing that the discussion between the four friends has thrown up is that there are many different ideas about God, and this affects our belief in God.

But before we think about this there is one matter which the friends didn't consider which needs to be mentioned.

The four friends' ideas about God were all moulded by the Christian tradition. We must not forget, however, that other religious traditions exist and that the friends could have met a few Muslims, seen a Buddhist monk in the street, and known a Hindu colleague at work. Though it has not been possible in this book to explore the religious experiences and ideas found in such faiths, they are, and will remain, very important. As it is, the friends' discussions have produced plenty to think about.[1]

Let us go back to chapter three. When Geoff asked Anne what she meant by 'God' she was flummoxed, and Tim tried to help her out by saying that we all know what we mean when we say we believe in God. On being pressed by Geoff, Tim declared that he certainly didn't believe in an old man in the sky. Cindy challenged this by pointing to the common Christian assertion that human beings were created in the image of God. She went on to suggest that since Christians call God 'Father', this must mean that God is imagined as a superior kind of man. Anne rejected the idea that God made us in his image, but admitted that she did think of him as human 'in a sort of way'. She expanded on this by proposing that God must be 'personal' or he would be less than a person. But she emphasized that he was 'spiritual', and that he was neither male nor female, although she conceded that she often did think of him as a man.[2]

And then there was Sarah. She had left the church because she believed that Christianity put women into subjection. A male God had an evil consequence. It meant that men were the

---

[1] See Peter D. Bishop, *The Christian and People of Other Faiths* in this series for a discussion of some of the issues that these other religions raise for the Christian.

[2] For a further discussion of the idea of the 'image of God' see the Appendix (p. 97).

rulers. She wanted a Goddess who was a woman with women. But she wasn't interested in a Goddess who was simply a female God. When she spoke of 'Goddess' she was referring to an attitude to the world, an attitude of liberation for all those who are being exploited. 'Goddess is an ecologically harmonious world. Goddess is creative self-expression,' she said. Anne didn't tell this to her three friends. Perhaps she should have done. But she probably thought it was so extreme that it would have diverted them from their proper discussions. We will come back to Sarah later.

Probably most of us think of God as Anne did. After all, it's very much the picture of God that we find in the Bible, and our hymns and prayers reinforce this image: 'Our Father, who art in heaven.'

Many Christians find such language sufficient. This is how Jesus taught us to pray. This is how Jesus spoke of God. This is how he addressed God in his own prayers.

So while they will almost certainly reject the phrase, 'an old man in the sky', and stress that God is spirit, essentially their idea of God is of a superior human being. They will affirm, in fact, that he is perfect in goodness since to his great power and knowledge – he can do anything and knows everything – is to be added his quality of being 'all-loving'. We may call it the God of the simple believer.

It isn't an image that should be easily pushed aside.

Cindy, however, told the friends that she had read some books on theology when she was in the sixth form at school, and knew that philosophers weren't satisfied with this way of thinking about God. They argued that God is so different from human beings that none of the words which we use for things on earth can apply directly to God. Rather we can only say what God is *not* – he is *not* physical, he is *not* limited in power or knowledge, he is *not* confined to space and time. Picking up Pascal's phrase, we might describe this picture as 'the God of the philosophers'. So here is another idea of God.

71

But there is more to be said about this idea. Cindy questioned whether we could say anything meaningful about God. She explained that philosophers sometimes tried to defend how we describe God by using the idea of 'analogy'. She gave the adjective 'friendly' as an example of what they mean, and used it of her neighbour, the dogs across the road, and a computer.

Cindy thought that because we don't know what God is actually like – whether God is more like a person than a computer, for example – anything we say about him is without any literal meaning. But perhaps the philosophers are too afraid of imagining God as just a superior human being. Tim's point seems to be valid. Persons are the highest kind of beings that we know, so that to think of God in any other way would be to make him *less* than human. But clearly he is much more than simply a superior human being.

So the idea of analogy should perhaps be considered further. Take one of the things that we say about God: he is 'loving'. We know what it means to love someone, but we cannot *know* what it means for God to love – not in the sense that we experience love ourselves and know what it means to be a person. We can only say that we believe God acts in the kind of way that if it were a human action we would describe it as loving. But this can have a real meaning.

Look at it like this. When we say James loves his son Peter, we mean that he enjoys being with him and sharing his activities, that they do things together, that he listens to what he has to say, that he was sympathetic when his girl friend threw him over and did everything he could to cheer him up, that he was desperately concerned when he caught meningitis, and so on. Now to say that God is loving means that he has *at least* all these feelings, even if he cannot do all these things because he is invisible and does not possess a human body.

That brings us to Anthony Freeman, the Anglican priest who denied that God 'exists' in the same way that things exist in the world. He found that he didn't believe in any kind of 'God out

72

there', any 'external God', any 'transcendent' God. None of the arguments for God's existence that we shall look at later cut any ice with him. Yet he found that *not* believing in God made no difference to the way he lived and the things that he regarded as important. He still believed in goodness and love and truth, and he was just as opposed to cruelty and suffering. So he retained the word 'God' for the sum of all his values and ideals. Language about God now had to present a way of life and to spell out its practical implications. Those who think of religion in this way often describe God as a 'symbol' – 'a symbol that represents to us everything that spirituality requires of us and promises to us', to quote from another philosopher who holds similar beliefs.[3]

Three of the friends regarded this as atheistic, since as Cindy expressed it, for these philosophers '"God" is a human invention'. Geoff's response, however, deserves to be considered carefully. He pointed out two important things.

In the first place, how you define 'atheist' depends on what your idea of God is. So that what we described as 'the God of the simple believer' might equally be called 'the God of the simple atheist'! But suppose that we doubt the possibility of articulating any idea of God. For language has grown through human interaction with the material world, and to say that something 'exists' indicates that we can see it, hear it, or detect it with scientific instruments. But God is not a *part* of the universe; and, if we cannot say anything that is *literally* true of him, how can we speak of him?

This leads to the second point that Geoff made. Writers like Anthony Freeman are absolutely convinced that living our lives in a good, truthful, and loving way is of supreme value. All the religions, they believe, are human creations – sets of ideas that human beings have devised and ways of life that the saints have practised. And because they are of supreme value, they function

---

[3] Don Cupitt, *Taking Leave of God* (SCM Press, 1980), 14.

for us as God. This is sometimes called a 'non-realist' view of God, because it does not accept a God who 'really exists', but nevertheless retains the conviction that the virtues which have been associated with religion in the past are of supreme value.

We must come back to Anne's friend Sarah. She left the church because she regarded Christianity as unredeemably patriarchal. When she and Anne had their chat in the coffee shop she set out the feminist criticism of religion and presented a feminist picture of God. This view of Sarah's is extreme, though it is one which has been accepted by several serious theologians and philosophers. Some comment is needed.

There is more than one feminist approach to the Bible and to the church.

Some feminists accept 'the God of the simple believer', but try to remove the 'sexist' features that they detect in Christianity, while still believing in God as our 'Mother and Father', or trying to work out other metaphors which do not express ideas that they find offensive and untrue. Some of the prayers that are used in church services nowadays are influenced by these ideas. For example, we might pray: 'Loving God, our parent, our saviour, God among us'. This goes further than simply using 'inclusive' language for human beings, and thinks of God in different metaphors and uses different analogies from those that have been traditional in the Christian church.

At the other extreme are those like Sarah, who reject Christianity and develop religions of 'Goddess'. They make a great deal of female experiences and the female body in their understanding of the world. Moreover they are somewhat similar to the 'non-realist' philosophers in denying that there is anything beyond our material universe, so that they find the essential features of religion in the kind of life that is lived here and now, a life of freedom for everyone.

74

Feminism, therefore, does not offer a fourth, quite separate image of God, but presents a special slant on the non-realist ideas that we have already examined. These feminists reject the idea of God as powerful in the sense that he has power over other people and other things and can control everything. They don't think of Goddess as a reversal of the male God, but still having a real existence outside the universe. Rather they are concerned with choosing to live in a way that is friendly towards the world with all its different peoples and animals. Often life after death is rejected, because the feminists are deeply concerned about the future of our planet, and they believe that an interest in a future life is a distraction and diverts us from making strenuous efforts to do something about pressing ecological issues. In much the same way that God (or Goddess) is interpreted as human choices and values, so immortality is seen as the elements in our bodies continuing in the natural cycle by decomposing and being reformed in plants and animals.

We see, therefore, that the question, 'Is there a God?' is far from simple. Even 'the God of the simple believer' covers a fairly wide spectrum of beliefs.

There are those who really do picture God entirely in human terms, the God who can work miracles, who answers prayer by doing what the believer asks, whether curing the illness of their loved ones or enabling them to win in competitive sport. Their God is usually held to be male, and some see the attempts to accommodate the concerns of women as pagan.

Most Christians probably regard this as extreme. Although they still think of God as personal, they accept that he is not literally a person. They pray to God as Father and don't consciously think of this as a metaphor, and they probably think of Jesus fairly literally as God's son. But like Anne, if they were pressed they would concede that we must think of God in spiritual terms. Other Christians may modify their ideas of God even more. Some feminists, for example, prefer to speak of God as Father and Mother.

Beyond this, however, we have noted 'the God of the philosophers' who is outside of space and time, who is changeless and eternal. He is real, in the sense that he is not simply a description of our highest ideals and virtues. But we can't know him as he actually is. And while I've used 'He' and 'Him' for this transcendent God, this is only because to say 'It' would make him lower than the highest human beings. In fact sex is not part of the being of God, and cannot be.

And there is the God of the Anthony Freeman (and others) who is a symbol for the sum total of all our virtues and ideals.

What has all this to do with the question, 'Is there a God?'? We shall consider this in the next chapter.

Questions for discussion

1. Which of the ideas of God that have been described in this chapter do you find convincing? Why?

2. How would you meet the charge that the God of 'the simple believer' is made in a human image?

3. How many of the things that you believe about God are metaphors? What do you think we can say about God that is *literally* true?

4. To what extent do you think that we should use feminine terms like 'Mother' for God?

16

Why Do You Believe in God?

The question 'Why do you believe in God?' can mean two things.

Most people, I imagine, take it to mean, 'What reasons can you give for believing in God?'. In other words, 'What arguments are there for believing that God exists?' But it can also mean, 'What led you to believe in God? What influenced you?'. The friends discussed both meanings, and it is worth looking at the second meaning before considering reasons for believing in God.

Anne was honest is saying that before Cindy had asked her why she believed in God she hadn't given the question any thought. She had been brought up in a home where her parents were Christians, and it seemed natural to take God's existence for granted. We might say that it was as much a part of her world as the sun, or the flowers in the garden. But she was also persuaded that Christianity was true because her parents were such wonderful people.

Tim's experience was similar. He believed what he thought the other people in church believed, and because going to church and taking an active part in what went on there boosted his ego, he saw no reason not to believe. He denied that he began to lose his faith because of Cindy's influence, though he admitted that it seemed less certain once his church attendance lapsed.

Most of us probably became believers in much the same way. There is nothing wrong with it. It's the way we learn most things, and if believing as a Christian is part of the make-up of people we love and admire, it is entirely natural. Tim's experience, however, must make us wonder how much of our faith is really conforming to what we think the other members of a group which we want to belong to believe and practise. Once we realize this, we may well begin to doubt. Indeed, doubting may be the first step in gaining a personal faith for ourselves, a faith that we can hold with a clear conscience. And remember that Tim said that he had thought more about God after he had stopped going to church than he had when he went every Sunday and several times in the week. It is worth thinking about.

Then there was Cindy. Her parents didn't go to church, yet they were wonderful people too. So they probably had an influence on her. But she claimed that what made her an atheist wasn't that, or at least not just that. Because she met so many Christian ideas all around her – we can think of such things as school assembly, the existence of church buildings, the main holidays at Christian festivals – she had assumed that all adults were believers, even if in a non-demonstrative way.

Then several things happened. First there was her father's illness, which made it impossible for him to play the piano any longer, and changed his personality, so that he became completely different from the great friend that he had always been. So the problem of suffering forced itself upon her. As she said, she decided that, if there was a God, he must be an absolute fiend to destroy her father like that.

Then she learnt about evolution and her biology teacher said outright that she didn't believe that there was a God. This widened Cindy's horizon and, in a way, eased her puzzlement and pain. She no longer felt, we may suppose, that she needed to explain why God had let her father suffer as he did.

But she wanted to pursue the matter further, and when she read the books on philosophy of religion, the arguments which were supposed to prove that there is a God seemed to her to do just the opposite. They were so unconvincing that they raised more problems than they were supposed to solve.

So why do you believe what you do believe? We will have a look at the traditional arguments for the existence of God in the next chapter. First I want to follow up what we have learnt about Anne, Tim and Cindy. They had all three moved from an unthinking faith, which had fully satisfied them, to questioning, doubt, and even outright atheism, and this happened for different reasons.

With Anne it was because Cindy had asked her why she believed in God and she found she didn't have an answer to the question.

Tim had taken his beliefs from the church circle in which he spent much of his free time, and when he was no longer carried along by his friends there he found that he began to have doubts.

Cindy had had to face the harsh fact of her father's illness, and this was coupled with discovering that there were some people who admitted that they were atheists.

Does this mean that faith in God is simply a matter of belonging to a particular group of people, who influence each other? Might we say, even, that for us God *is* that group of people? This hardly seems adequate, but it's worth remembering that we hold many of our ideas simply because people around us hold them as well – or even, as Geoff commented, because we *think* they hold them!

But if faith itself has no firmer ground than that the people around us hold it, the possibility is clearly open that we are all deceiving ourselves, and we cannot be happy to leave such a hope unresolved. We need, therefore, to think things through, asking once again why we believe in God.

Anne tried to find the answer in religious experience, and this is probably the first thing that many people will think of. The trouble was that she hadn't ever had one! Or at least the experiences that she had once had seemed to her to be no more than bursts of emotion. The friends recalled some of the experiences that other people had reported. One of their church members had described how he talked to Jesus as he drove to work. A former minister had told them of the way Jesus had appeared to him. Fred had spoken of a sudden sense of peace that came over him just after his wife had died and he knew that

God was there, holding him in his arms. I invented Fred's experience for the sake of the discussion. The church member was a Reader in an evangelical Anglican church that I know. The minister is Ronald Dale, and he describes this and other experiences of Jesus in his broadcast talks and his books. We might go on. Bishop Hugh Montefiore was born a Jew. He tells us in his autobiography that he was sitting in his study at Rugby school when suddenly he became aware of a figure in white, who spoke the words, 'Follow me.' He says, 'Instinctively I knew that this was Jesus, heaven knows how: I knew nothing about him . . . it was an indescribably rich event that filled me afterwards with overpowering joy . . . I found that I had become a Christian as a result of a totally unexpected and most unusual spiritual experience.' It controlled his whole life.

It is not only Christians who have had religious experiences. James Laver, who was Keeper of the Print Room at the Victoria and Albert Museum, tells of an occasion during the Second World War when he was at a cinema and in the film a woman stood on a terrace in the moonlight. As he watched her he heard a voice saying quite distinctly, 'If that is the beauty of mortal woman, what must the beauty of Holy Wisdom be!' The glow of the experience remained with him during the whole of a long, cold train journey back to London.

Claims to have had religious experiences have been collected and analysed by scholars. It has been suggested that such experiences fall into five types: (1) experiences like those which Anne and James Laver had: something non-religious leads to a mystical experience; (2) unusual experiences which are 'public' in the sense that more than one person has them; (3) private experiences, such as the appearance of saints or angels or Jesus in dreams or while awaking – Ronald Dale and Bishop Montefiore are examples; another slightly different example is Marietta Jaeger, whose seven-year-old daughter was kidnapped and murdered: when she was questioning what kind of a God would allow such a dreadful thing to happen, she suddenly felt, almost   physically, a sense of God's love embracing her; (4) experiences that those who receive them find it impossible to describe in everyday language and which may include a sense of being at one with the entire universe or being caught up into God: these are often called mystical experiences; (5) an inner conviction, perhaps that a loved one who has died is safe with God, or that a course of action must be followed, as when a minister feels he or she has a 'call' to the ministry, even though they hear no audible voice.

These experiences carry great conviction with those who have experienced them, and even if second-hand accounts of such experiences don't seem to have the same impact as one's own experience, they have to be taken seriously. So many people claim to have had them, with life-changing results, that they cannot be lightly dismissed.

Nevertheless, there are serious difficulties in taking religious experiences as proofs of the existence of God. They may have had physical causes. The fact that 'mystical' experiences have been induced by mescaline cannot do other than raise a certain scepticism, though those who accept that they are genuine experiences of God would claim that God revealed himself through the physical. Those who had the experience may have misinterpreted what they saw or heard or felt. Anne questioned whether the mystical experience she had had might have been simply an emotional reaction to the beauty of the hills and the shadows of the evening sun. In worship the experience may have been induced by the fervour of the preaching or the hypnotic effect of choruses.

Those who have had experiences which they interpreted as experiences of God are left with no doubts at all, and the effects of their experiences often continue into their later life. But those who have never had such experiences may find it difficult to regard what others have felt as a proof of the existence of God. And certainly we cannot base our belief in God solely on the experiences which other people have had.

This is probably especially disconcerting to Methodists, who have been brought up on John Wesley's experience of a heart 'strangely warmed' and the doctrine that all those who are 'saved' can know that they are saved.[1] Nevertheless, it is difficult to avoid the conclusion that there are some people who want to believe and have never had a religious experience that confirmed their faith. We must be honest about this. Many sincere Christians have not had any such experiences, mystical or other.

In the end it seems that we must admit that all that we can do is to accept that many people have had unusual psychological experiences which they have interpreted as experiences of God or of saints or angels. As we might expect, they find these experiences totally convincing. We can't move beyond this. The sceptical Thomas Hobbes commented that 'though God almighty can speak to a man by dreams, visions, voice, and inspiration; yet he obliges no man to believe he had done so to him that pretends [claims] it; who (being a man) may err, and (which is more) may lie.' This is unduly cynical and is expressed offensively, but the point is sound. In the end there appears to be no way to decide between two possibilities: that the experiences (or some of them) derive from God, or that all 'religious' experiences have a natural explanation.

Questions for discussion

1. What led you to believe in God? Share your experiences with the group?

---

[1] I am aware that John Wesley changed his mind about 'assurance'. At first he thought that all genuine Christians would experience assurance, but later he accepted that many saints didn't. Nevertheless, in popular Methodist thought the first two items in the 'Methodist Quadrilateral' are: 'All can be saved; all can know that they have been saved'.

2. Examine your reactions to the experiences that are described in this chapter.

3. Consider the implications of the two possibilities that are mentioned in the final paragraph.

17

The Traditional 'Proofs'

In the discussion between the friends we have met two of the so-called 'Proofs' for the existence of God that have been developed by philosophers. We can call these (1) the argument from the definition of God, (2) the argument from the wonderful order in the universe. (The technical names for them are the Ontological Argument and the Teleological Argument.) The friends discussed them pretty thoroughly, and it is only necessary to set out the arguments rather more systematically.

The argument from the definition of God

Cindy presented this argument in the form that was set out by Anselm (1033–1109).

He first of all defined God as 'that than which no greater (i.e. more perfect) can be conceived'.

He then distinguished between an imaginary God, who exists only in our minds, and a real God, who actually exists.

But, he argued, an imaginary God is less perfect than a real God.

So, if God is 'that than which no greater can be conceived', he must exist.

The friends agreed that this seemed to be an unconvincing argument, and Cindy gave the counter argument that a contemporary of Anselm's, a monk named Gaunilo, offered. He pointed out that Anselm's argument would be absurd if you applied it to anything else, such as the most perfect island. To this Anselm replied that his argument only applied to God, because the idea of the most perfect island does not include its existence, while our conception of God does.

Although the argument has fascinated many philosophers and attempts have recently been made to show that it has some force, Geoff showed where it fails (re-read pp. 20–28). But he also showed that it pointed to something that is important in our

84

idea of God. If your little nephew asked you 'Who made the world?' you might answer, 'God.' But what if he then asked, 'Who made God?' You'd have a job to explain it to your little nephew, but the answer is that one of the things about being God is that no one made him. If he didn't always exist he wouldn't be what we mean by God. So although the argument can't prove that there actually is a God, it shows us that part of what we mean by 'God' is that he exists 'eternally'. He didn't come into existence, and no one 'made' him.

Of course, you can't go on from that and argue that because the universe exists, there must be a God who created it. It might be that the universe just exists as brute fact, and we can't say why it exists. It might have always existed and will always exist. (One scientific theory – not accepted by the majority of scientists – is that the universe is eternally expanding out of the compacting of all energy into one point – the singularity – and then when it has reached a certain size contracting back into that point again, when the whole process starts again. Whether that is right or not, we have no means of knowing scientifically what happened 'before' the 'big bang' that seems to have started off the universe as we know it. And since time did not exist until after the 'big bang' the question doesn't make much sense anyway. Some scientists and theologians are willing to speak about what lies 'behind' the universe, stressing that 'behind' doesn't mean 'before' it 'began'. They then argue that it is God who is behind it .)

The argument from the wonderful order in the universe

Anne had heard of Paley's watch. The passage is so famous that it deserves being quoted:

> In crossing a heath, suppose I pitched my foot against a *stone*, and were asked how the stone came to be there; I might possibly answer, that, for anything I knew to the contrary, it had lain there for ever: nor would it perhaps be very easy to show the absurdity of this answer. But suppose I had found a *watch* upon the ground and it should be inquired how the

watch happened to be in that place; I should hardly think of the answer which I had before given . . . [for] when we come to inspect the watch, we perceive (what we could not discover in the stone) that its several parts are framed and put together for a purpose . . . [and so it must have been made by a watchmaker].

Paley goes on to point out that the argument holds even if we had never seen a watch before, if the watch we found didn't work perfectly, and if we didn't know what the purpose of the watch was. He also said that even if we discovered that this watch had been made by an earlier watch, we should still want to go back to an original watchmaker of the first watch in the series. And he denied that we could possibly suppose that the watch had just come together by chance. He went on to point to the way the eye is perfectly designed for seeing, birds' wings for flying, the shape of fishes for swimming, and so on.

It is an argument which most of us have found impressive at some time or other, and the more intricate and wonderful we discover the universe to be, the more it seems to point us to a creator. But the theory of evolution dealt the argument a death blow, for instead of the characteristics of birds and fish being part of God's deliberate design, they are now seen to have evolved through natural selection.

The underlying fault of the argument is that its strength depends upon the extent to which the universe is like a watch. It is an argument based on the analogy between the watch and the universe. If the similarity is not close, then the analogy is faulty and the argument fails. And evolution, apparently driven by chance events, makes it very difficult to claim that the universe is like a watch.

It might be possible to rescue part of the argument by pointing out that the universe contains more order than it might otherwise have done, sufficient order, in fact, to enable the appearance of human beings with minds and consciences. Yet the sceptic will remain sceptical. Cindy referred to the 'Blind Watchmaker', which is the title of a book by Richard Dawkins.

He argues that chance acting cumulatively can bring about change which is apparently purposeful and so there is no need to posit an intelligent creator. And even if the believer suggests that God used evolution as the means of creating the universe, this fails to persuade the sceptic, for he replies that it is possible to understand the evolution of the world as entirely due to chance, and in any case natural selection means that the changes were due to physical causes and not the direction of a hidden creator. If the believer replies that God must have been directing the process because, instead of reverting to chaos, everything became wonderfully complex, the doubter will still claim that we don't need to find a reason for the way things are, but must simply accept what happened.

It is at this point that some scientists enter the discussion, as Geoff pointed out. It appears that during the first few minute fractions of a second after the 'big bang', scientific laws were established which made it possible for the universe as we know it to evolve and for life to arise on at least one planet attached to a star. If the fine tuning had been only very slightly different the universe would have collapsed into itself or would have expanded rapidly without the stars forming, and therefore without the carbon molecules on which life depends being created. The likelihood of this happening by chance is judged to be so remote that these scientists and their followers see it as a firm argument for the existence of a God who designed a universe in which it was possible for human beings to appear.

We need to be careful about this argument. Ours is the only universe that we know, so that we can't tell whether it is only one among a vast number of universes. We wouldn't be here if it wasn't just the right kind of universe in which life was possible. We have then to decide which is more incredible: that there should be countless universes among which ours is the only one that we know, or that there is an intelligent creator who 'fixed' the laws of nature so that our universe evolved as it did and life became possible on our planet. And there is always the possibility that one day scientists will discover why the events in the first fraction of time after the 'big bang' had to be as they are. We need to be careful not to make the same mistake about the 'fine tuning' of the universe – what philosophers have called the 'anthropic principle' – as Paley did about the intricate design that he saw in the world. Believers have always been too ready to bring in God to explain gaps in their knowledge.

There is a further difficulty. Even if God is needed to provide the 'fine tuning' in the first fraction of time in the life of the universe, this is not sufficient to prove that he is the kind of God the religious believer desires and loves. At most he is a great mathematician. The presence of evil, and especially the evils that are inherent in evolution, is a strong counter-argument. A fantastically intelligent Mind with no concern for morality is hardly the Christian God – or the God of any of the great world religions.

Anne wondered why there is the universe and not just nothing, and I imagine that we have all wondered about that at some time or other. Notice that we aren't asking whether there was a 'first cause' which started off the whole chain of causes that bring us from the 'big bang' down to the present. The question is: How pressing do you find the mystery of the actual existence of the universe? Why does it exist when it might not? If we find its existence puzzling, we then have to ask which is most convincing: (a) the universe just exists and we have to accept that fact, or (b) the exceeding complex universe which human beings have discovered through the use of their minds must have a mind behind it.

The first view points up several important features about belief in God. One of the difficulties about claiming that God is the maker of the universe is that we are using the words 'maker' and 'exists' in different ways from the normal way we use them. Time and space only began after the 'big bang'. They are features of the universe, and only exist within it. So it makes no sense to ask about what happened 'before' the 'big bang'. There wasn't a 'before' because there wasn't any 'time'. In the same way 'making' things only belongs to relationships *within* the universe, and to say that God 'made' it is using the word 'to make' in a different way, a way that we cannot give a meaning to. As we saw in chapter 15, attempts have been made to overcome this by describing the link between what we say about things in our world and the nature and activity of God as 'analogy', but this fails to meet the key problem. We don't know in what ways the words have a different meaning when they are used of God.

Another difficulty is that because all our thinking takes place within a world of space and time, we cannot imagine what a being who exists outside of the universe would be like. Look at it this way. Suppose you were a being that lived only on a flat page, so that your whole existence was like what we would call a picture. You would be quite unable to imagine what solid beings like dogs and horses and human beings were like. And although you knew what a square was, you would not be able to think of a cube. It wouldn't do to say it was a square only infinitely 'squarer'. To you 'up' would mean moving from the bottom to the top of the 'picture'. You wouldn't be able to conceive of moving 'up' from the surface of the page, and to say it was 'up' taken to a much greater degree would be meaningless.

In the same way, we cannot possibly imagine what a timeless God who 'exists' outside of space can be like. Indeed, it is impossible for us to give any real meaning to 'exists' when we use it of God, for to us, everything exists because it fills a space in the universe and continues through time.

Finally, as we have seen, this 'First Cause', this 'Maker' of the universe cannot himself (or itself!) be created by anything else. It cannot be possible for him *not* to exist. And that again is an idea that we find it very difficult to comprehend. He would be radically different from anything else within the universe.

This isn't necessarily an objection to the argument, for if God is to be God, he must be beyond our comprehension. As a great mystic once said, 'A God who can be comprehended is no God'. The more transcendent God is, however, the less we are able to say about him, and every human argument for his existence falls.

We might conclude that it is easier and simpler just to accept that the universe exists as brute fact. This isn't the end of the story, however, for human beings have managed to learn so much about our complex universe by using their minds, that to say that the electrons and the other particles that form matter are all that exists seems inadequate. Mind and spirit exist as well.

Conclusions

We have picked up only two arguments. Several others have been proposed by philosophers, and those who are interested can read about them in the suggestions for 'Further Reading'. It is time, however, to collect up our thoughts about the arguments that have been set out here.

In the first place, it has to be stated clearly and firmly that no knock-down argument for the existence of God which will convince the hardiest sceptic has been discovered, and it is certain that none will appear in the future. The reason is quite simple. It is always possible to adopt the materialist position that all that exists is the physical universe. There is no need to explain it. Indeed, it is impossible to do so. We just have to accept it as brute fact.

Moreover, the arguments for the existence of God, even if they were valid, point to a God who is much less than the God that religious believers require. The 'Unmoved Mover', 'the First Cause', the 'Designer' – I use the names that the philosophers have coined – are all far removed from the God who acts as a Father and Mother and who can be described as perfect love. This God would be even further away from the Christian God who revealed himself in Jesus.

Perhaps, then, we may feel that Geoff was right in suggesting that the friends may not have been on the right track. Away with the arguments and simply trust in God! Or rely on religious experience. And yet . . . Even if the arguments don't convince the sceptic, they have a value in showing believers that their faith is not irrational.

That is the point of that curious argument about other minds. None of the friends was really convinced with the argument Geoff put forward, partly because they did not quite see the point. He wasn't offering yet another 'proof' of the existence of God. Rather he was suggesting two things. In the first place, a *weak* argument is different from a *bad* argument. The arguments for the existence of other minds and the arguments for the existence of God are both weak, but neither are bad arguments, and we shouldn't reject them because they aren't strong arguments. Secondly, he wanted to turn the emphasis away from questions of 'proof' to the question of 'rationality'. Granted that believers don't come to belief through intellectual argument, what matters is whether belief in God is rational or not.

Perhaps this is more important than it might appear at first sight. We have seen that *how* we come to faith is usually because of our parents, our families, our friendships, membership of a church, and so on. But unless we are simply going to believe what our friends believe, or what we think they believe, or believe on purely emotional grounds, or believe because of our need to belong to a group, we need to assure ourselves that believing in God is rational.

The faith of the greatest of the saints and the most advanced of the mystics is that of trustful children, and cannot be anything else. And the arguments of the greatest human thinkers are feeble gropings. So when we have said all that we can, and stretched our minds as far as they will reach, we have only touched the hem of God's garment. We end our intellectual search in a metaphor. How else can we speak?

Questions for discussion

1. Which of the arguments seems most convincing to you. What is there about it which you find persuasive?

2. The argument that the fine-tuning of the universe was necessary if human life was to appear has been called the 'anthropic principle'. Consider whether it is self-centred because it regards the purpose of the existence of the gigantic, expanding universe as simply to make human beings possible.

3. Does it matter whether faith is rational or not? Why?

18
Revelation

The friends were surprised when Geoff said that they hadn't mentioned the Trinity in their discussions. When they talked about it the next week, they found that what they were really discussing was whether God revealed himself to human beings and, if so, how he did it.

The group decided that one way in which God revealed himself was through individual religious experience, and we have already considered that (see chapter 16). But on the last evening in their series of talks together, they wondered what place Jesus had in their faith.

Geoff confessed that he found it very difficult to think of Jesus as any more than a human being. He didn't want to press his ideas on the others and recognized that they would need to look again at the Gospels to think about Jesus properly. But he admired Fred, who believed that God revealed himself to us in Jesus and acknowledged Jesus as his Lord, and accepted that orthodox Christianity held that Jesus, the chief channel of revelation, was 'the Son of God'. He couldn't go as far at that, but allowed that, if it is true, the main reason for believing in God would be that he has revealed himself to us.

There are, however, a great many problems with the idea of revelation – too many to discuss in this short book. Here only three things can be mentioned.

(1) First, Geoff's inability to accept that Jesus was God makes clear that the appeal to revelation is no more conclusive than the proofs for the existence of God. It provides material for reflection and, in the end, we have to decide what we make of it. We may not like the way that Pascal's wager depicts it. We may reject the idea that you can will yourself to believe or simply decide to believe. We may, with Tim, think that the wager offers a pretty selfish reason for believing in God. We may find Studdert Kennedy's version of the bet more attractive and true to life. Whatever our reaction,

revelation faces us with a decision rather than provides a solution.

(2) Secondly, there are problems about both the acceptance and rejection of the Christian revelation.

(i) The friends, rejecting what they took to be the biblical view of a God who is constantly interfering in human affairs, working miracles for those who are his favourites, went on to explore 'the God of the philosophers'. It may seem that a recognition of the transcendence and mystery of God – as Meister Eckhart said, 'a God who can be comprehended is not God at all' – is very sensible. For if we knew all about God he would be no greater than us. But, granted that God must be mysterious, is it at all possible to claim that he is active in the world? Clearly, the concept of 'providence', which we here touch on, is as important as it is difficult. But it is hard to distinguish between a God who is so distant that he doesn't act in any discernible way in our world and no God at all.

(ii) If, on the other hand, we accept the Christian revelation, philosophical discussion may seem unnecessary. If all – or at least all that we need for living the Christian life – has been revealed in Jesus, the search for 'proofs' of God's existence seems misguided, and many Christians appear to be satisfied with this conclusion. But they live among unbelievers, and ought to be able to defend their faith. Everyone ought to ask whether they can 'give a reason for the faith that is in them'. If they don't face up to this challenge, their faith may be no better than superstition. We may find it unsettling to ask questions about our faith, but since Christians accept that Jesus called on his followers to love God with their *minds*, they ought to be prepared to think things through.

(iii) The Christian revelation isn't the only one now presented to us. Judaism, Islam, Hinduism, Buddhism, Sikhism, and other world religions offer alternative views of God. Faced by their claims and contributions, it is more difficult to affirm that God revealed himself only in Jesus and that answers to all our problems can be found by coming to God through him. Certainly, it would be unwise, in our present situation, to dismiss the God of the philosophers as dramatically as Pascal did.

(3) The third problem about making revelation central is that no revelation is perfect. It simply is not sufficient to say that Jesus is the complete revelation of God. He lived two thousand years ago in a foreign country and within a different culture. We cannot be certain about what he actually said. Some of the things told about him look like legends. Everything we know about him was passed on to us by his disciples, and they may have misunderstood him. Down the centuries some Christians have certainly misunderstood the revelation, as the burning of heretics and the waging of crusades show.

So we shouldn't dismiss the God of the philosophers too readily. Although the four friends often found church services embarrassing, they were all helped by discussing ideas contributed by philosophers. So they decided to continue their meetings. Although Fred never joined the friends in their discussions – he probably regarded such debates as a waste of time compared with active Christian service – he was always in the background. And his faith shouldn't be dismissed as an unexamined faith. He had thought it through and now simply wanted to live it out.

Once again we come back to the question of whether faith is reasonable. Many Christians are quite content to believe without examining their faith, and find support in the church services they attend and the Christian groups to which they belong. Should their faith be disturbed? Isn't it better to believe than to lose every foothold in life?

Such Christians will not read books such as this. But if, by any chance, they do, they will see, I hope, how important it is to examine our faith, no matter how painful the process may be. Cindy, you will recall, asked Anne why she believed in God. Because Anne couldn't answer the question, the friends began to discuss it together, and, if we are to be honest with ourselves and with other people, it is a question that we too must face as squarely as they did. Our answer may not lie exactly along the path that the friends travelled. Perhaps, however, their journey may offer some help.

As for the four friends. Anne and Geoff still attend their church every Sunday and take a full part in its activities. Cindy and Tim have been to several different churches. They feel most comfortable in the Friends Meeting House, but they are also often to be found in an Anglican church which has Matins every Sunday.

The friends still meet in each other's homes every week, and some of their friends now join them. They find that there are many things about religion that they want to go on discussing.

Questions for discussion

1. What are the differences between the God of the philosophers and the God of Abraham, Isaac and Jacob . . . and Jesus?

2. 'An unexamined faith is no faith.' But what if the examination is disturbing?

3. Where do you find the greatest help in your religious life?

Appendix

The 'Image of God'

Sarah parodied the idea that human beings were made in the image of God and declared that the doctrine really meant that Christians create God in their own image (pp. 11–12). There is probably something in this, but it is unfair to many Christians and fails to take account of a long tradition within Christian theology. On the other hand, the idea is often trotted out thoughtlessly in order to support some ethical position, such as opposition to abortion or euthanasia. Some would say that, by sharply separating human beings from the rest of the animals, the doctrine has hindered Christian opposition to such practices as the ill-treatment of calves and pigs in factory farming, and the keeping of battery hens, as well as the use of animals in medical research, practices which they hold to be evil.

In this short appendix only three points can be made.

1. It is striking that two verses, almost unique in the Old Testament, have been given such prominence in theological thought. 'Then God said, "Let us make human beings in our image, after our likeness . . ." So God created human beings in his own image, in the image of God he created them; male and female he created them' (Genesis 1.26–27). Apart from the reference back to these verses in Genesis 5.1 and 9.6, the reader of the Bible has to turn hundreds of pages before finding another reference. Historically the earliest mention of the divine image is in Ben Sirach (Ecclesiasticus) in the Apocrypha, where the writer looks back to Genesis 1: 'The Lord created man out of the earth, and turned him back to it again . . . He endowed them with strength like his own, and made them in his own image' (Sirach 17.1, 3). Paul holds the same belief, though in a patriarchal way, declaring that men (males) ought not to cover their heads when praying because they are 'the image and glory of God' (1 Corinthians 11.7). More distinctively, however, he fastens on Christ as the image

of God (2 Corinthians 4.4; Colossians 1.15, cf. Romans 8.29; 1 Corinthians 15.49).

The idea of humans beings created in the image of God is hardly a central *biblical* belief, and it needs to be recognized that the doctrine developed largely within the Christian church. How far this was a legitimate development might be debated.

Certainly there runs through the Bible a belief in the clear difference between human beings and animals. One scholar has even argued that according to the Old Testament the Israelites treated domestic animals simply as 'superior tools' – tools that had to be looked after and protected, but nevertheless existed solely for the benefit of their owners. Apart from the attitude of Jesus, the same appears to be true of the New Testament as well. Paul notoriously quoted 'You shall not muzzle an ox when it is treading out the grain' (Deuteronomy 25.4) to defend supporting those who proclaim the gospel, and asked whether God was concerned for oxen (1 Corinthians 9.9).

2. It is important to remember that the phrase, 'God created human beings in his image' comes from a narrative which all scholars would describe as myth. Few Christians today regard Genesis 1–11 as literal history. Like Anne, they accept that human beings appeared on this planet in the course of a long period of evolution, and that the discovery of DNA has shown how closely they are related to the rest of animal creation. The trouble with constantly reiterating the claim that human beings have been *created* in the image of God is that it gives the impression to those outside the church that Christians *do* believe that God created the world as described in Genesis, and are therefore benighted fanatics who hold to an outlandish superstition.

Two important consequences flow from the understanding of Genesis 1–11 as myth and the acceptance of evolution. (a) In the first place, many Christians would wish to stress the *religious* value of the Genesis stories. They see here important truths about the relation between human beings and God, and the nature and effects of sin. To take the stories literally and then demand that they should be abandoned because they conflict with science seems to them to misunderstand the kind of writing that they are. So they would defend the idea of 'the image of God', not just because it is a part of scripture but much more because of its religious teaching. (b) Secondly, the fact of evolution has to be taken in all seriousness. If human beings evolved through the process that scientists describe, there was no Fall and much of the theology that is grounded on the acceptance of an original state of innocence, a Fall, and the reversal of the Fall in the salvation brought by the 'Second Adam' needs to be expressed in different ways.

3. Much of the discussion of Genesis 1.26–27 has been concerned with how the 'image' is to be understood and in what way human beings are 'like' God. Again there is no space here to discuss the distinction, first made by Irenaeus in the second century, between 'image' and 'likeness'. This distinction, which is not intended in the original Hebrew story, persisted up to the Reformation and is still maintained in the Orthodox Church, and led to questions being asked whether the image or the likeness was lost in the Fall. The likeness to God has usually been thought of as spiritual qualities or capacities, although other suggestions about the meaning of the phrase in Genesis have been made, such as that human beings are God's counterpart, or that they are God's representatives on earth (in the same way as the king was regarded Yahweh's representative in ancient Israel, or the image of the ancient Middle Eastern monarch represented the ruler himself in countries he had conquered).

In summary, the idea of 'the image of God' rests on very slender biblical evidence. Emphasis on the claim that human beings have been created in the image of God is open to serious misunderstanding today, and may lead to harmful consequences through the rigid separation between human beings and the animals which it implies. Most human beings, however, including many Christians, regard themselves as 'higher' than the animals, so that they 'matter' far more than animals do. For this reason they would accept the use of animals in medical research, provided that there is no deliberate cruelty and suffering is kept to a minimum. Some of those defending animals rights would disagree, of course.

On the other hand, provided that it is recognized that the phrase is a metaphor for the idea that human beings are capable of entering into a spiritual relationship with God, it can offer important teaching about the position of human beings in the world. It is because there is a similarity between human beings and God that prayer is possible. And even if the idea of ethics as the imitation of God is not found extensively in the Bible, Christians today may see themselves as called to reflect God's loving concern for the animals in the way they treat them.

In all this, however, we must be careful not to take 'made in the image of God' as if it brings God down to our level. To that extent Sarah was right. The discussions in chapters 3 and 15 show that how we think of God is central to any debate about his existence. Overemphasis on the image of God can easily distort our thinking by suggesting pictures of God that are all too human. 'The God of the philosophers' is not to be quickly pushed aside. A God who can be fully understood by human beings is no God at all.

Further Reading

Most of the books on the philosophy of religion include chapters on the traditional proofs. Three may be particularly recommended, although several others might well have been added.

David A. Pailin, *Groundwork of Philosophy of Religion* (Epworth Press, 1986).

This is clear and well written. Besides a chapter on 'Faith and the Existence of God', there are useful discussions on such issues as faith and reason. It is an admirable introduction to most of the philosophical issues.

Stuart Brown, *Philosophy of Religion: An Introduction with Readings* (Routledge, 2001).

Stuart Brown is a professor of philosophy at the Open University, and this book was devised for 'entry-level students'. In accordance with modern educational theory, 'Objectives' are set out at the beginning. There are questions, exercises, summaries, and readings from classical texts. You will either greatly enjoy this approach or be irritated by it.

Peter Vardy, *The Puzzle of God* (Fount, expanded edition, 1995).

What is of particular interest about this book is the account of four different views of God: the 'Timeless God', the 'Everlasting God', 'Talk of God as Talk about an Alternative Lifestyle', and the anti-realist view of 'God as Reality within a Religious Form of Life'. The writing is very accessible and down to earth, and the discussion is lively and related to the ways people normally think.

Among books dealing with the traditional proofs two can be noted:

J. H. Hick, *Arguments for the Existence of God* (Macmillan, 1970).

Although an older book, Hick writes extremely clearly. This is probably the best single book devoted entirely to the traditional proofs.

Anthony Kenny, *The Five Ways* (Routledge & Kegan Paul, 1969).

This also is an older book. The 'Five Ways' are the arguments which Aquinas put forward for the existence of God, as the subtitle explains. The discussion is carried on at the level of high philosophy.

Two books deal more generally with the question of the existence of God and are less tied to the traditional proofs:

Richard Swinburne, *Is There a God?* (OUP, 1996).

This comes at the end of a series of books that Professor Swinburne has written on religious belief and the existence of God. His aim is to present a positive case for God's existence, and he takes account of Richard Dawkins's *The Blind Watchmaker* and Stephen Hawking's *A Brief History of Time*.

Garth L. Hallett, *A Middle Way to God* (OUP, 2000).

This is the most recent exposition of the argument that belief in other minds and belief in God are equally rational. Not all will be convinced, and some may regard it as as presenting a curious approach. Even if the two beliefs are on a level, so what?

Those interested in Anthony Freeman's non-realist position (which is largely derived from the ideas of Don Cupitt) may like to read his own account and a reply by Richard Harries:

Anthony Freeman, *God in Us: A Case for Christian Humanism* (SCM Press, 1993).

Richard Harries, *The Real God: A Response to Anthony Freeman's* God in Us (Mowbray, 1994).

Feminist writings proliferate at an ever expanding rate. One of the most recent that deals with the question of the idea of God is:

Mary Grey, *Introducing Feminist Images of God* (Sheffield Academic Press, 2001).

This is in the series 'Introductions to Feminist Theology'. Mary Grey sets out the objections of many feminists to traditional Christian attitudes towards God and ways of speaking of 'Him', and describes various feminist ways of thinking of God/Goddess, including a Christian trinitarian belief. It contains a large bibliography.

There is an equally vast literature on the 'image of God', both within Old Testament study and by theologians. Three books which may be obtained from libraries contain useful discussions.

Claus Westermann, *Genesis 1–11* (SPCK, 1974).

In a discussion of Genesis 1.26–28 (pp. 147–161), which contains a long excursus on the history of interpretations of these verses, Westermann provides a very full and clear exposition of the different ways in which the passage has been understood.

Geoffrey Wainwright, *Doxology: The Praise of God in Worship, Doctrine and Life* (Epworth Press, 1980).

In this systematic theology, based on its expression in liturgy, Wainwright devotes a whole chapter (pp. 15–44) to the image of God. He finds three strands in the doctrine: the human vocation to communion with God (prayer and worship); the human task upon God's earth (the care of the natural world); and the construction of humanity as social being (notably within the church).

Anthony Hanson and Richard Hanson, *Reasonable Belief: A Survey of Christian Faith* (OUP, 1980).

Sharper and more radical than either of the other two discussions, the short account by the Hansons (pp. 135–139) interprets the image as the moral freedom which human beings possess, and which distinguishes them from the animals.